HOW TO ORGANIZE AND RUN A FILM SOCIETY

How to Organize and Run a Film Society

JANET WEINER

THE MACMILLAN COMPANY, New York, New York

COLLIER-MACMILLAN PUBLISHERS, London

The Macmillan Company
866 Third Avenue, New York, N.Y. 10022
Collier-Macmillan Canada Ltd., Toronto, Ontario
Library of Congress Catalog Card Number: 72-80071
First Printing
Printed in the United States of America

To Michael, who got me the contract;
to Russell Goldencloud, who
played by my side while I wrote

Contents

HOW TO ORGANIZE AND RUN A FILM SOCIETY

1

Overview

THE FIRST PUBLIC SHOWING OF MOVING PICTURES WAS IN 1895, when the Lumière Brothers staged their performance of this new media in the basement of the Grand Café in Paris. Only a few paying customers were on hand to witness it.

By 1915 motion pictures had become a booming industry. Theaters were under construction all over the world to accommodate the increasing demands of spectators. Movies were "big business."

Though motion pictures were originally dismissed as nothing more than a passing fad by artists, writers and critics, the year 1915 found the industry attracting many of these same people—people with talent and imagination who had finally recognized the potential for artistic expression inherent in this new invention. D.W. Griffith was giving us *The Birth of a Nation*, earning himself recognition as the first really great artist of the industry. By 1914 Charlie Chaplin had established himself as a comic genius, not only to those who went to see his films for entertainment purposes but also to people who were looking to cinema for something more, as an expression of artistic creativity and feeling.

A distinction between movies became possible: those that were made strictly as business properties and those, made as a commercial property or not, that contained elements that lifted them to the level of art. Cinema as business or cinema as art. People became interested in studying and discussing the artistic films, and their interest led to the formation of groups for such purposes.

The very first film society was formed in Paris in 1920 under the direction of Louis Delluc. By 1925 there were groups in Australia, Canada, England, France, Germany, Scotland and the United States. Their aim generally was to screen movies not regularly shown in the commercial theaters. While they of course recognized the fact that films of artistic merit were being shown in the commercial cinemas, they concentrated their efforts on screening films produced outside Hollywood and the major film industries of other nations—films that were being ignored, neglected and left to die as "non-commercial properties." Movies by such people as Denmark's Carl Dreyer, Sweden's Victor Sjöstrom, Russia's Sergei Eisenstein, France's René Clair, Germany's Fritz Lang had audiences outside their countries of origin largely through the sponsorship of film societies around the world.

When sound pictures were introduced, a new problem for the film industry evolved, and along with it a new market was created for film societies. The silent foreign film was universally understood and its few titles were easily translated, so there were no problems with international distribution. Foreign films with foreign *dialogue* were unwelcome to the general public. Consequently, commercial exhibitors shied away from screening these money losers. The members of film societies strongly supported their local groups' efforts to present these foreign-dialogue films, especially when the society was located in a metropolitan area, with a more sophisticated audience. Subtitling and dubbing foreign-language films has been common practice for some time. Good titles are in such demand now that many are placed into commercial-theater distribution immediately after screenings at the major European film festivals. Today in the United States a substantial number of foreign-language films are still premiered by film societies. Most groups also include classics of the golden age of silent film, classic comedies and films of the Thirties and Forties in their programming. However, the emphasis now is on contemporary cinema. Films made and distributed by small independent companies are in great demand by film societies across the United States. Some groups have been so successful with their programming that they have formed "art" theaters where the patronage is large enough to support such ventures. Still, the average film-society membership is about 300 to 500 persons, and it is groups of this size that now prevail. The nationwide audience for film-society screenings is estimated at about five million.

In general, then, a film society provides an alternative in movie entertainment that is not usually available in commercial theaters. The overall effort is film for the sake of art rather than for business purposes.

Film-society formats can vary endlessly. Almost any film is available for rental in 16mm, excluding new releases on the theatrical circuit, which are generally available six months to two years after initial release. For convenience, areas of interest are arranged around the following themes:

(1) The premiering of new independent productions, both American and foreign. Very often the director or producer of these films doesn't want the property exhibited theatrically and would rather have it viewed by the people who are most capable of giving it fair appraisal. That these titles are not in commercial distribution is no judgment on their quality. Even if the film-makers would like to see their titles have a theatrical run, the major commercial distributors and studios generally ignore them unless they have had some financial or contractual interest in a film since its inception. Ernie Pintoff's *Dynamite Chicken* and Peter Watkins' *The Gladiators* are two examples of films in this category. The market for films produced by independent companies outside the major commercial movie industry is an ever more popular one.

(2) Rerunning popular films previously screened in major commercial theaters, both American and foreign titles, for study in retrospect or strict entertainment. Studios such as Cinema V, Columbia Pictures, 20th Century–Fox, United Artists and Warner Brothers, for example, are finding the 16mm non-theatrical market so profitable that they now release their titles to film societies and schools six months to two years after initial commercial release. *Joe, Death in Venice, Woodstock, Z, The Conformist* and *Little Big Man* were all released in 16mm no later than eighteen months after their first commercial run.

(3) Revival of classics, comedies, serials, other oldies and films from the silent era—Charlie Chaplin, W.C. Fields, Flash Gordon, Fritz Lang and Busby Berkeley films, for example.

(4) Foreign and American classics from the Thirties, Forties and Fifties—films such as *Citizen Kane, The Treasure of the Sierra Madre, 8 1/2, Seven Samurai, The African Queen*, etc.

Many societies draw upon all these areas of interest when selecting a program; others choose one approach and stick to it. Very often a society's program is dictated by its finances. Popular films have high rental rates; obscure titles rent for less. New-release films are more expensive than films that have been out one to two years. Feature film rentals vary anywhere from $7.50 to thousands of dollars, depending on the title, the audience and the admission charge. (Detailed programming suggestions are enumerated further on in this volume.)

Good relations between film societies and distributors is highly important. Distributors should be treated very well indeed. They should be paid accurately and on time, and their films should not be mishandled, mutilated or, regretfully, stolen. Mistreatment of a distributor can make things more difficult for *all* film groups.

Furthermore, as an exhibitor of 16mm non-theatrical films, a society has the responsibility to support the smaller distributors of independent film-makers' work. These companies are American Documentary Films, Canyon Cinema Co-Operative, Creative Film Society, EYR Campus Programs, Genesis Films, Leacock-Pennebaker, Newline Cinema and News Reel Films. These companies often obtain the rights to distribute excellent American and foreign productions that are not distributed by the larger studios. By booking these titles a film society is fulfilling its time-honored function: premiering new works of cinema that would otherwise be ignored. In the case of the cooperatives especially, the film-maker's share of the rental is very good. Obviously, the more money he has to work with, the more he can produce. Cinema as independent art rather than studio business is further promoted. The benefits to the film society for supporting these distributors are substantial. They generally respond more quickly to booking requests and, unlike the more commercialized non-theatrical distributors, they are more willing to allow multiple exhibition without increasing the rental rate. If your group is based on a college or high-school campus you will very likely have a more successful season choosing films predominantly from these companies. Contemporary cinema has enormous appeal on campuses nationwide.

These smaller distribution companies can survive only if you support them by renting their titles and pay them what they are due. Hopefully they will not only survive but continue to prosper and grow to a point where they have such a selection that it will become unnecessary for you to deal with the very commercialized 16mm distribution companies whose main interest is charging whatever the traffic will bear.

Organizing and maintaining the operation of a film society is quite a complicated affair, and indications are that the job will never be any easier, only increasingly difficult. However, it can be an enjoyable one for both organizer and patron. There is a feeling of relaxation and together-ness at screenings that is not so readily achieved in commercial movie houses. Many communities have only their local college or high school to rely on for any sort of cultural activity. A stimulating film program can go a long way toward filling the need for entertainment. In cities, film societies are especially valuable because they provide an atmosphere of film appreciation rather than of film consumption only.

People like to bring their kids, their dogs, smoke, hang their feet on the chair in front of them, discuss the film with the manager, tell the projectionist when the sound is too low, linger afterward to discuss the film—in other words, to enjoy themselves.

All in all it can be a very relaxed and pleasant kind of experience. Hope-fully this book will tell you what you need to know to lessen the strains of operation and increase the pleasure of running a film society.

2

Organization

A FILM SOCIETY CAN BE DEFINED AS "A NON-PROFIT CULTURAL organization formed to encourage the appreciation of cinema both as an art and as a medium of information and education, by means of showing films, discussing them and supplying its members with information about cinema."

A more functional definition would be: "An organization formed specifically for the purpose of presenting a film program on a regular basis."

Should you wish to have a formal constitution, the following will be helpful:

Suggested Bylaw (Constitution) Provisions for a Local Organization

Article I NAME

Article II PURPOSES
(If the purposes are stated in a charter, they need not be repeated in the bylaws.)

Article III MEMBERSHIP
A. Classes of membership with eligibility requirements, rights and privileges of each class (active, associate, honorary, etc.)
B. Requirements of parent organization if group holds a charter from higher organization
C. Procedure for membership application and certification

5

Article IV   OFFICERS
    A.   List of officers of organization
    B.   Method of selection
    C.   Duties of each officer

Article V   BOARD OF DIRECTORS
    A.   Membership
        1.   Ex-officio members (usually the officers of the organization)
        2.   Elected members: qualifications
    B.   Officers of board
        1.   Qualifications
        2.   Selection
    C.   Duties and responsibilities of board (usually the duty and power to act for the organization between meetings of the organization)
    D.   Executive committee of board
        1.   Membership
        2.   Duties
    E.   Meetings of board
    F.   Reports of board and executive committee

Article VI   MEETINGS
    A.   Annual: notice, business to be conducted, order of business
    B.   Regular: notice, usual order of business
    C.   Special: how called, notice

Article VII   COMMITTEES
    A.   Standing committees: list of standing committees, number of members, selection, duties, powers, meetings, reports
    B.   Special committees: provisions for selection

Article VIII   FINANCES
    A.   Budget preparation and adoption
    B.   Dues: how determined, when delinquent
    C.   Auditor: how selected, type of report
    D.   Surety bond for officers and employees

Article IX   TERMS OF OFFICE
    A.   Length of term of officers and board members
    B.   Staggering of terms

Article X   ELECTIONS
    A.   Time and method of nominating
    B.   Nominating committee: duties and report
    C.   Time and method of election
    D.   Vote necessary to elect

Article XI   QUORUM
    A.   Meetings of organization
    B.   Meetings of board

Article XII   DISCIPLINE AND EXPULSION OF MEMBERS
    A.   Grounds for action

Some sort of formal constitution is usually necessary, and filling out the preceding bylaw provisions step by step will provide a simple, clearly understood guide that will suffice for most situations.

Chances are the idea for the society has been generated by one person, so the first thing to do is to find a few other people (minimum two, maximum four, including yourself) who are also interested in showing films and to decide among you who is to be chairman, secretary, treasurer, et cetera. *You can't do it alone.* Neither can it be done with ten or twenty or thirty people having a voice in every small decision. The smoothest-running groups are those in which one person is ultimately responsible for the financial stability of the organization. Many arguments will be avoided if you decide in advance that the chairman you've chosen is the final authority.

After this, you'll want to decide what type of format you're going to present. The more competition there is, the more specialized the format must become. Just because there are ten art theaters, five film societies and eighteen commercial movie houses in one area does not mean the field is saturated. There are so many varieties in programming (see Chapter 4) that it is quite unlikely that every possible format has been spoken for. You'll be going at the project with new advertising, new enthusiasm and lots of energy that will interest people and draw them to your activities. Creating high expectation and then living up to it is the trick.

One positive factor about starting a film society where there are others in existence is that you *know* you have a probable audience that could financially sustain your club. All that's necessary is the right films, organization and promotion.

Assuming there is a chairman and one to three other persons who will work with him, and you've thought out the direction you want to follow in programming, you should pick your first three films. This may seem a bit hasty, but it is not. Prints of 16mm films are in such high demand that it is essential to plan far ahead.

After you've received the confirmation for the first title, go ahead and rent the auditorium that has been chosen during the time you've been waiting for replies from the distributors.

In choosing an auditorium, your first consideration must of necessity be availability. Finding a hall you can use on a regular basis with the security of some form of agreement guaranteeing you the rights to the place on a certain night or nights during the week is essential. Next is projection facilities. A good sound system and good acoustics are quite important. Try to pick a hall that holds at least 150 people, for each time a film is shown the rental fee is generally increased by 50 percent. If you expect 500 people and have a 500-seat auditorium, you can show the film once at, for instance, a $250 base minimum guarantee. If the auditorium holds 250, the film will have to be shown twice, and the rental fee jumps to $375. The projectionist must also be paid more money for more hours worked. There is possibly a higher fee for the facility for two screenings instead of one. Of course if the expected attendance is estimated at a total of 200 to 250, a larger facility is not desirable. In usual circumstances where the audience varies from week to week, the more seats the facility has, the cheaper the show will be to finance.

If the group is based on a college or high-school campus, there shouldn't be too much trouble in finding an adequate facility. Community organizations should check out meeting halls, churches, barns, warehouses, the local schools' auditoriums and/or cafeterias. Quite possibly there is a community theater whose facilities can be rented when not in actual production.

During the time that a suitable screening location is being sought, you will contact people who might be interested in the group. Those who express enthusiasm should be invited to the very first meeting you hold after the organization is more or less under control.

Before the first screening, frequent meetings are necessary. The most important item on the agenda at these meetings is advertising. The designing of the promotional material and its circulation are of vital importance. Directly after confirmation of film and auditorium has been attained, a handbill should be designed and distributed as widely as possible. The more people who know about the film, the larger the audience will be. A comprehensive advertising program is equally important to the selection of the right title.

After a routine has been established, a weekly meeting will allow enough time for discussion of most matters. Some groups find it easiest to hold their meetings the evenings of the screenings. If the film is scheduled to begin at 8:00 P.M., the meeting can be called at 6:00 P.M., leaving an hour and a half to get through all details. This is also a convenient method for insuring members' cooperation with the physical running of the show. Since they're already there, why not stay and help out?

However, the time when meetings are most important is *before* your first screening. There will be so many unfamiliar details to be worked out that thorough discussion is mandatory. Even if only two executive members get together, one of them is bound to think of some problem that hasn't been satisfactorily solved. Even if everything *is* running smoothly, the other person acts as a sounding board, and it can be very reassuring to tell each other everything that has been done to date.

Important Things to be Scheduled:
1. Film bookings
2. Hall bookings
3. Advertising (allow two weeks)
4. Projection equipment rentals
5. Triple-checking on film arrival
   (More detail on these points later)

If you've got the above five areas under control, things should go smoothly. Advance planning is absolutely essential. It isn't unusual for a film society to have an entire year's program booked in advance—auditorium *and* films. Careful planning will also save duplication of effort. Knowing *who* is going to do *what* and *when* is half the battle. A weekly work list can be drawn up as follows: (Many of these tasks can be accomplished using less time than indicated below—for instance, one trip to the printer per month instead of twice a week.)

SUNDAY

MONDAY
1. Pay bills
   a. film rental
   b. previous week's costs
2. Finish putting up film announcements
3. Bank deposit
4. Design handbill for following week's show to be printed
5. Public service announcements

TUESDAY
1. Take next week's announcement for printing
2. Check for film arrival
3. Check film announcements

WEDNESDAY
1. Call distributor if Friday's film has not arrived
2. Check film announcements
3. One or two hours devoted to writing for catalogues, reviewing film magazines and new catalogues. Making film bookings for future months

THURSDAY　　1. Call projectionist to verify Friday night
　　　　　　2. Check announcements

FRIDAY　　　1. Call at printer for next week's film announcements
　　　　　　2. Check tonight's show film announcements
　　　　　　3. Double-check equipment
　　　　　　4. 6:00 to 7:00 P.M. meeting
　　　　　　5. 7:30 to 8:00 P.M. setup
　　　　　　6. 8:00 to 10:30 P.M. show

SATURDAY　　1. Post next week's film announcements
　　　　　　2. Mail film back

Draw up this kind of schedule at least one month in advance. In this way the work can be divided. Each person will know his responsibilities in advance, and last-minute hysteria will hopefully be avoided.

As the success of a film society depends mainly on the choice of film, a research committee should be established immediately. Their duties will be to:

1. Get catalogues from every 16mm distributor in the country. (See names and addresses, Chapter 8)
2. Keep up to date on new releases by reviewing newspapers, film periodicals and other magazines, such as:
   Film Society Review, 144 Bleecker Street, New York 10012
   The Village Voice, 80 University Place, New York 10003
   Film Quarterly, University of California Press, Berkeley, California 94720
   Film Heritage, Box 652, University of Dayton, Dayton, Ohio 45409
   Films in Review, National Review Board of Motion Pictures, 210 E. 68th Street, New York 10021
   The Silent Picture, 613 Harrow Road, London W. 10
   Sight and Sound, 155 W. 15th Street, New York 10011
   Take One, Unicorn Publishing Corporation, P.O. Box 1778, Station B., Montreal 110
   Monthly Film Bulletin, British Film Institute, 81 Dean Street, London EIV 6AA (available also from *F.S.R.—Film Society Review—*with *membership*)
   Rolling Stone, 746 Brannan Street, San Francisco 94103
   Cinefantastique, 7470 Diversey, Elmwood Park, Illinois 60635
   New Cinema Review (film-makers newsletter), 80 Wooster Street, New York 10012

Film, 72 Dean Street, London W.1

Cineaste, 144 Bleecker Street, New York 10012

Film Comment, 100 Walnut Place, Brookline, Massachusetts 02146

Canyon Cinema Newsletter, 263 Colgate Avenue, Berkeley, California 94708

International Film Guide, Tantivy Press, 108 New Bond Street, London W.1

Interview, 10th floor, 33 Union Square West, New York 10003

Afterimage, Narci's Publishing Company 12/13 Little Newport Street, London WC2H 7JJ

Film Fan Monthly, The Silent Picture, 613 Harrow Road, London W.10

Focus on Film, Tantivy Press, 108 New Bond Street, London W.1

On Film, subscription service, P.O. Box 10044, Kansas City, Missouri 64111

Film Facts, P.O. Box 213, Village Station, New York 10014

Variety, 154 W. 46 St., New York 10036

These subscriptions should be made as soon as possible. If you're short on funds, at least subscribe to *Film Society Review* and *The Village Voice.* The information contained in these two periodicals is very up to date, the former for film distributor information, the latter for ideas of what to run, reviews to films.

Establishing a filing system right from the outset won't hurt. With so many titles to think about, this can insure that information someone has researched isn't discussed and then forgotten. You can devise a very simple system. All you need are two index card boxes and 3 x 5 file cards.

#1

FOR FILMS

TITLE _____   Distributor _____

RENTAL FEE: $_____   Director: _____

REVIEWS   PICTURES
(list publications)   List publications and/or
                         books containing clip from ad
_____   and page reference (indicate
_____   here if catalogue contains
_____   satisfactory advertising)

Date Rented: _____

#2

FOR DISTRIBUTORS

DISTRIBUTION COMPANY _____

Date to write for
new catalogues:

_____

Latest catalogue: _____.
Releases known through 197_____.

FILMS RENTED:

_____

_____

_____

As each film periodical and catalogue arrives they are reviewed and logged in the above system. You won't want to record every title, only those that are of potential interest.

The chairman, as coordinator of all activities, will probably also select the film program, after the research committee suggests tentative titles and submits their recommendations. (More detail in Chapter 4.) He, together with the secretary, will have to devote a good deal of time, well in advance of the beginning of a season, to writing distributors and securing *definite* confirmations of films, dates, rental prices and method of shipment.

Second only to the choice of films and promotion the success of a society is determined by reliability. If you start a reputation of no-shows, you'll very quickly find people reluctant to come again. Once burned, twice shy. The only way I know to insure that every film will arrive on time is to be *fanatically* explicit with distributors concerning method of shipment and how far in advance of play dates they will ship the films. Don't let this slide. Write them as many times as necessary to receive this essential information.

Since the executives of a film society may change from year to year, it is vital to keep records of the following, in *one* place, usually with the chairman:

Film catalogues, film filing and distributor filing systems
Film periodicals and newspapers
Minutes of meeting
Checking-account records, check and deposit slips
Attendance report and financial summary for each show
Tax payments
All correspondence
Membership list
List of places the society advertises their films
Equipment (spare bulbs, etc.)

Taking care of important tasks *in the proper order* is never easy when it's all new. Keep in mind the most essential points: 1) the film; 2) a place to show it; and 3) advertising the show. All the other details will fall into place around these three main tasks. In time, a routine will be established and the work can be accomplished with a minimum of wasted energy. But in the beginning, plan on spending as many hours as necessary.

3

Finances

FILM SOCIETIES ARE NON-PROFIT-MAKING ORGANIZATIONS. However, the very nature of the activities of the club dictates the need to handle things on a businesslike basis. The money to rent films has to come from somewhere (usually admissions, or subscription memberships), and the survival of the organization depends directly on its financial soundness.

Officers of film societies contribute their time voluntarily. They cannot receive a salary for the executive functions performed as chairman, assistant chairman, secretary or treasurer. There are several paid positions in the organization. The projectionist receives a salary on an hourly basis. Whenever surplus funds permit, the people responsible for putting up the posters should be paid for this work. Sometimes it is necessary to hire an artist or layout person to design the promotional materials. Paid secretarial help can prove invaluable during high-peak work periods. Whenever the occasion arises where an executive of the club is filling a function usually paid for by the club, such as projectionist, cashier or ticket taker, he is eligible to be paid for the time spent at these normally paid positions.

If a particular season program is very successful, the members may vote the person in charge of picking the films a bonus honorarium, something akin to paying him for services as a booking agent. However, the club is not a business, and executive officers, members and the club itself cannot make a legal profit.

FINANCING THE FIRST SCREENING

An initial investment of $300 to $500 is usually necessary. If your group is a college- or high-school-based club, you might be able to secure a loan or grant from the student union. When this is not possible, another method would be to borrow the necessary funds from three or four individuals who want to see the club get started. If all goes well, their faith will be rewarded and you'll be able to repay them within a month.

If you're a community-based organization you might seek a loan or outright grant from a cultural-advancement institution, or the community chest in your town. If this fails, you can approach individuals and/or some small established businesses in town whose owners would be willing to take the risk of loaning you $50 to $100 apiece. There is every likelihood you'll be able to reimburse them within one month.

It is very difficult to solicit subscription memberships prior to the first show, simply because people are reluctant to buy a season pass from an unproven organization. The subscription membership drive should be launched at your first screening, should you choose to finance the club that way.

WEEKLY EXPENSES

For purposes of lending some reality to the following sums of money, we'll create a hypothetical film society—call it the Cinema Group. They are a student–faculty group and screen their films on the university campus, one show Thursday and another show Friday. Their auditorium seats 275 persons comfortably, and the weekly attendance figures average out to 500 persons (taking the season as a whole). They charge $1.25 admission.

A.	Average weekly *film rental*	$250.00
B.	*Promotional* materials	
	1. Flyers (500 copies photo-offset)	12.50
	2. Supplies (glue, paper, dry-transfer letters)	5.00
	3. Percentage of season announcement cost	6.00
C.	*Hall* rental ($20 per night)	40.00
D.	*Projector* rental: (two 16mm projectors at $7.50 each per night)	30.00
E.	*Shipping* to and from distributor (air freight)	45.00

F. *Advertising budget*
    1. Paid help   15.00
    2. Newspaper ads (when permitted by distributor)   10.00
G. *Program notes* (mimeographed)   2.50
H. *Projectionist*
    Two and one-half hours per night at $2.50 per hour
    equals $6.25 per night   12.50
I. *Miscellaneous*
    1. Projector *bulbs* ($.30 per hour per bulb)   1.20
    2. *Tax* on gross admissions (4%)   25.00
    3. *Telephone* and long-distance calls   7.50
    4. *Stationery, stamps, gasoline, film cleaning,*
        minor equipment   15.00
    5. Magazine and *periodicals—subscription fees*   5.00

                                                                   TOTAL $482.20

The Cinema Group spends $482.20 weekly and takes in $625 weekly. Their club is ahead $142.80, on the average. Some films will lose that much, and others will make more.

Most distributors now demand payment in advance of the shipping date of a film. Thus, at the beginning of a season, the society will have already paid out several advances totaling hundreds of dollars and will still have to come up with the extra money for an adequate promotional campaign, advance auditorium rentals and other things. The tension will ease after a few shows when hopefully there will be enough funds to have paid off the outstanding debts and have some surplus money remaining.

As it is necessary to continue paying film rentals in advance (until you've established credit with distributors who will trust you), it is advisable to maintain as high a bank balance as possible. Not having the money to pay for a film in advance will certainly cause severe problems.

But you cannot be so paranoid about reserve cash supplies that you refuse to spend on the "extras" which make your club special. These extras include advertising, which should be as sophisticated as possible and printed on fine paper; the inclusion of short subjects, cartoons or serials to accompany your feature films; long-distance phone calls that may cost $10 but which are sometimes essential in booking a film; complementary passes; attractive membership cards; file cabinets; and even office space.

All of these things cost, and of course most of these extra expenses are not usually necessary at the outset of the first season. The frills will seem important later, once the group is firmly established.

What admission should be charged? Film societies charge from $.50

to $2 per person. Children under twelve are often admitted at one-half price. The most usual admission fees are $1 to $1.25.

Determine the admission by taking the following into consideration:

A. Your expenses
B. Your anticipated attendance (figure low)
C. Admission charged by nearby commercial theaters
D. Admission charged by other groups in the area

You might decide to begin by charging $1.50 admission but soon find your attendance better than was expected and drop the fee to $1.25. Conversely, if you begin by charging $1 and continuously have to struggle to make ends meet, you might raise the fee to $1.25, which is not very much more per person, yet yields an extra $25 per hundred customers.

It all depends on the situation. Charging $1 to $1.50 on a university campus would be acceptable. At high schools, charge $.50 to $1, depending on the film.

For community groups wishing to supply family-type entertainment at a moderate cost, charging $.75 per adult and $.50 per child would be all right with most people.

You must be very careful to follow the restrictions enumerated by the distributors with whom you're working. Many of them absolutely prohibit the film being advertised to the general public, insisting that notices are to be placed only on the high-school or college campus where the film is to be shown. Other companies won't allow single at-the-door admissions to be charged, demanding that only members of that specific film organization be allowed to attend. Be sure to write the distribution company in full detail regarding how much you're going to charge and whether or not the patronage will be members only or the general public. This will save grief later on, as local theater owners have been known to complain bitterly when they feel their business is being taken away. At a few state colleges the state legislators, responding to the pressures of local theater owners, have even prohibited the existence of film societies.

Obviously, then, it's a good idea to get along with your local theaters. When they are playing a good film, tell your customers about it. It's not going to take any of your business away, and it goes a long way toward cementing friendly relations.

There are plenty of distribution companies whose films are never exhibited in commercial theaters; hence their restrictions are practically nonexistent. They encourage advertising the films by every available method and often will supply newspaper advertising materials and radio spots specifically for that purpose, in addition to finely designed posters. Newline Cinema, EYR Campus Programs and Genesis Films are the best of these companies. All three are a pleasure to work with. Theater owners don't usually mind competition from this direction.

SUBSCRIPTION MEMBERSHIPS

The most desirable situation is where you can get about 500 people to purchase a season ticket, providing them with a fair discount. This will give the organization the security of having all the necessary funds to finance the entire program in advance.

If your season has a total of fifteen play dates and you're charging $1.25 admission, the total cost for a person attending each screening would be $18.75. You could offer the entire season at a price of $15, thus saving each subscriber $3.75, the cost of three admissions. This would give your organization a $7,500 budget for the season. Expenses for the fifteen weeks (based on the estimated expenses listed previously) would total $7,233. This leaves $267 surplus for emergencies that do arise. You can continue to charge at-the-door admission for those people who attend only one or two films a year and would never think of subscribing to fifteen films. Occasionally, when you think you'll have enough room, you might invite each member to bring along a guest for free. This doesn't cost you anything and helps to increase membership by interesting new people who may have never come in contact with film groups.

Some groups, seeing that no one is responding to their campaign to pay for fifteen films in advance even when they know they might attend every one, offer a different approach: purchase a three-film ticket for the price of two and one-half admissions—applicable to any of the films in the program. This is a small enough amount of money, and three films are more immediate than fifteen, so results may come flooding in. Also this can be handled at the door rather than by mail.

When you offer subscription memberships you should make every attempt to give as much information as possible about your organization —who's behind it, how the money is spent, how the films are chosen. The films, though, are the thing. As much detail as possible for each film —pictures, reviews, story plots, awards, actors, directors, cameramen, etc. —should be included. (More detail for this type of promotional campaign is available in Chapter 5.)

PLANNING YOUR BUDGET

As soon as you have received confirmations for all your films you can chart a realistic budget. Since the film rental is the lion's share of the weekly expenses, it's very difficult to figure out how much each show will cost until you know this figure.

A simple sheet can be made up as follows:

Film title: _____   Date(s) of screening(s): _____

Distributor: _____   _____

Admission charged: _____   Number of performances: _____

Expected attendance: _____

COSTS

		Projected	Actual
1	Film rental		
2.	Shipping from		
3.	Shipping to		
4.	Hall rental		
5.	Flyers		
6.	Percent of season promotional		
7.	Projector rentals		
8.	Projectionist		
9.	Tax		
10.	Program notes		
11.	Telephone		
12.	Other paid help		
13.	Stationery and stamps		
14.	Miscellaneous		
15.	Miscellaneous		
	Total		

Expected attendance _____ at $_____ admission equals
$_____ income (anticipated).

Projected expenses subtracted from projected income yields profit/loss (expected).

Actual Attendance Report
(to be completed after show)

Attendance show #1_____
Attendance show #2_____
Total _____ at $_____ = $_____

Minus   Gross receipts
        Expenses
        ‾‾‾‾‾‾‾‾‾‾‾‾‾‾‾
        Equals Profit

_____ (Or)

Minus   Expenses
        Gross receipts
        ‾‾‾‾‾‾‾‾‾‾‾‾‾‾‾
        Equals Loss

As you can see, this budget sheet serves a twofold purpose. After the showing of a particular film, it becomes the financial report for that week.

In order for a group to survive, it *must* maintain financial solvency. If you are particularly worried about the ability of your group to draw enough customers to pay for the rental and all other expenses, you might try writing distributors about a "no minimum" arrangement. In such situations, the distribution company receives approximately 85 percent of the gross receipts, the group retains 15 percent. But all risk on your side is eliminated.

Pay your bills on time. In this way when you need credit in a pinch, there is more likelihood of getting it.

A film society that can't support itself doesn't always mean there is a lack of interest or of potential customers. The choice of films might be poor, or the promotion campaign has been weak. Audience feedback can generally clue you into what's wrong. If the general consensus is that there is *nothing* wrong, the group will have to reduce expenses by renting cheaper films and eliminating some other costs (which might also cut the attendance) or give up the group altogether. Very often there is no time to figure out what's wrong. The first shows have been run and the club is in debt. So please be sure that you're running the right film and that your advertising is reaching the right potential audience.

4

Selecting Film Programs
and Booking the Titles

FILM SELECTION PROCEDURES

This chapter is perhaps the most important in this book. Either the selection of a program is good or it is bad. The success or failure of the group depends upon programming. The most vital point to remember is to research what films your potential audience wants to see.

Earlier I suggested that you pick three films and book them immediately even before renting an auditorium. This is really important, for 16mm non-theatrical exhibitions have increased so much in the past few years that the demands placed on prints of the most popular films have resulted in these titles becoming solidly booked for as much as six months in advance.

I would strongly suggest you pick your first three titles, after checking out local preferences, from the following listings (for college film groups):

AMERICAN	INDEPENDENT
Little Big Man	*Five Summer Stories*
Butch Cassidy and the Sundance Kid	*Gimme Shelter*
	Hendrix at Berkeley
The French Connection	*Easy Rider*
Midnight Cowboy	*THX-1138*
Straw Dogs	*Dynamite Chicken*
Andromeda Strain	*The Last Picture Show*
Klute	*The Hellstrom Chronicle*

FOREIGN	CLASSIC
Z	Original *Tarzan*
Death in Venice	*Reefer Madness*
Fellini Satyricon	*The Gold Rush*
If . . .	*The Blue Angel*
The Devils	*Flash Gordon*
Walkabout	*Conquers the*
Yellow Submarine	*Universe*
8 1/2	Dick Tracy Serial

All three of one area, or one of each area—it doesn't much matter. These films have all been very well received. They're crowd pleasers, with the exception of *The Devils*, which is X-rated, a brilliant film but brutal. However, brutality notwithstanding, or perhaps *because* of it, it did very well on its commercial run. Another reason I suggest these titles is that they are virtually surefire winners. When you are first beginning a film society you can't afford to pick films just a handful of people want to see for art's sake alone, unless the group is completely subsidized and it doesn't matter if no one shows up as *paying* customers.

If you can manage to launch the program on good financial footing you should be able to maintain the organization's self-supportive ability through the season.

Based upon the film selection procedures outlined by the Canadian Federation of Film Societies, the following guidelines should be discussed before you pick your program:

(1) One person, usually the chairman, should be given the authority to have the final veto or acceptance of film titles. He should further be allowed to make any last-minute changes without consulting the other executive members. Emergencies do arise. Substitutions sometimes must be arranged for.

(2) The research committee should gather together all the catalogues, film periodicals and new listings. Go through them making notes as to what is available that they think might do well.

(3) The lists of films the society has shown in past years should be resurrected, along with their financial summaries. You may want to rerun a film that was particularly successful. Usually there is a rapid changeover in film-society membership, so films shown previously are likely to be unseen as yet by the majority of this season's audience.

(4) Don't be frightened by the fact that a film you want to show has recently been screened by a commercial theater in your locale on a second run. But please never book a flick *only* because it has recently been in the

theaters. That is no guarantee at all that it will be successful—or that it is any good.

(5) Impress on the research committee members the idea that they are selecting films for the bulk of the members and not titles that they would personally like to see.

(6) If you are scheduling for fifteen dates, draw up a list of potential titles (forty or fifty films) from everyone's selections. Make copies and ask that the lists be shown around to friends, family, teachers, anyone at all. Ask these people to indicate their preferences and if possible get their suggestions for films they'd like to see which aren't on the list.

(7) At your next meeting the chairman, or program director if you have one, should be presented with the comments and suggestions and left to the task of picking the schedule, after the individual committee members have each submitted a preferred list.

(8) A word of caution: Watch the TV listings and try to obtain advance notices from the networks for their proposed movie schedules. No one wants to pay to see a film screened for free the night before in their living room.

(9) From these possible selections, pick out about half the number (in the case of a fifteen-film season, eight) of primary titles you want to show, the only criteria being that these films are important, well known, good-drawing titles. If there's margin for doubt as to whether one film is a better artistic choice than the next, choose the one with the larger draw. These eight will form the financial base of the entire program, and they must be selected carefully. They should be scheduled for every other week, starting week one with the title that has the best potential draw.

(10) Now fill in the gaps. Look at your choices from a point of balance. If you have picked a lot of comedies, you need dramas, adventure films, Westerns. You may have chosen mostly foreign films. If so, you need to add some English and American titles. If you have selected many recent films, add one or two classics and maybe some animation, or a program composed entirely of shorts.

(11) Go through the compiled list of possible selections again, with these blanks in mind as criteria of choice for your secondary selections. You may find yourself choosing a slightly inferior film, but don't be concerned as long as it adds a new element to the entire program.

(12) Alternate your secondary choices. Try to achieve an interesting variety between old and new, serious and funny, native and foreign. Your aim at this point is to add spice and artistic merit to what otherwise might become too commercialized a fare.

(13) Keep the list of alternates handy! In case you need to substitute

a title at the last minute later on in the season, you won't be caught wishing you'd made notes when all the possibilities were being discussed.

(14) Show the completed list to the research committee to check for any negative reactions, which should, of course, be attended to. The chairman should have ultimate say. He cannot allow the list to be torn apart and reconstructed every five minutes, but neither can he be allowed to ignore good sound criticism.

(15) Perhaps at this time, now that you have a list of films, you might draw up the budget sheets for each week. You may find you can afford to rent a film which is very high-priced and you didn't think you could handle. Only if the other titles are suitable in price can you allow for an extravagance.

(16) Leave an open date in your program, toward the end, for a film that may become available in the middle of a season.

(17) After the list has been completed you will want to select shorts to accompany at least some, if not all, of your films. A show running over two and a half hours becomes tiresome. If the feature is lengthy, eliminate the short.

Due to the high costs of film shipments (unless you ship via 4th class), whenever possible you should seek to book both feature and short from the same distributor. Both films can be packed in the same shipping case, and this will save you some money. Cartoons, serials, newsreels, underground shorts, mini-documentaries and travelogues—the variety is overwhelming.

(18) Familiarize yourself with what is available locally, or at short notice. (United Films in Tulsa, Oklahoma, and all the Swank Motion Picture offices are often willing to ship out titles the same day they're called long-distance, provided a print of the film desired is in stock.) You may have to make a substitution as late as the day before the scheduled show.

SAMPLE PROGRAMS

A.   Primary Films: *Straw Dogs, Gimme Shelter, Hendrix at Berkeley, Sweet Toronto, Midnight Cowboy, Butch Cassidy and the Sundance Kid, Brand X, Woman in the Dunes*

	VARIATION	VARIATION
1. *Straw Dogs*	1. *Straw Dogs*	1. *Straw Dogs*
2. *Fellini Satyricon*	2. *If . . .*	2. *Tricia's Wedding and Lenny Bruce on TV*

3. *Gimme Shelter*
4. *Death in Venice*
5. *Hendrix at Berkeley*
6. *The Conformist*

7. *Sweet Toronto*
8. *The Devils*

9. *Midnight Cowboy*
10. *Z*
11. *Butch Cassidy*
12. *The Confession*

13. *Brand X*
14. *Medea*
15. *Woman in the Dunes*

3. *Gimme Shelter*
4. *8 1/2*
5. *Hendrix at Berkeley*
6. *THX-1138*

7. *Sweet Toronto*
8. *Flash Gordon Conquers the Universe*

9. *Midnight Cowboy*
10. *Putney Swope*
11. *Butch Cassidy*
12. *The Gladiators*

13. *Brand X*
14. *On Any Sunday*
15. *Woman in the Dunes*

3. *Gimme Shelter*
4. *The Gold Rush*
5. *Hendrix at Berkeley*
6. *The Treasure of the Sierra Madre*
7. *Sweet Toronto*
8. *Even Dwarfs Started Small*

9. *Midnight Cowboy*
10. *The Gladiators*
11. *Butch Cassidy*
12. *Never Give a Sucker an Even Break*

13. *Brand X*
14. *Destry Rides Again*
15. *Woman in the Dunes*

B. Primary Films: *Little Big Man, The Clowns, The Andromeda Strain, 2001: A Space Odyssey, Death in Venice, The Devils, King of Hearts, THX-1138*

	VARIATION	VARIATION
1. *Little Big Man*	1. *Little Big Man*	1. *Little Big Man*
2. *Loves of a Blonde*	2. *Macunaima*	2. *Underground Festival of Shorts*
3. *2001*	3. *2001*	3. *2001*
4. *Seven Samurai*	4. *Blue Water, White Death*	4. *Paths of Glory*
5. *The Clowns*	5. *The Clowns*	5. *The Clowns*
6. *When Comedy Was King*	6. *Joe*	6. *The Hellstrom Chronicle*
7. *The Andromeda Strain*	7. *The Andromeda Strain*	7. *The Andromeda Strain*
8. *The Incredible Shrinking Man*	8. *Tristana*	8. *Bonnie and Clyde*
9. *Death in Venice*	9. *Death in Venice*	9. *Death in Venice*
10. *Klute*	10. *A Man Called Horse*	10. *Summer of '42*
11. *The Devils*	11. *The Devils*	11. *The Devils*
12. *Glen and Randa*	12. *Rosemary's Baby*	12. *Yojimbo*
13. *King of Hearts*	13. *King of Hearts*	13. *King of Hearts*
14. *Treasure Island*	14. *Days of Thrills and Laughter*	14. *Carnal Knowledge*
15. *THX-1138*	15. *THX-1138*	15. *THX-1138*

C. Specialty Programs
   1. Foreign film festivals
      a. (featuring films from many different countries):

   1. *The Wild Child* (France)
   2. *Death in Venice* (Italy)
   3. *The Conformist* (Italy)
   4. *My Night at Maud's* (France)
   5. *The Damned* (Italy)
   6. *Elvira Madigan* (Sweden)
   7. *The Passion of Anna* (Sweden)
   8. *Claire's Knee* (France)
   9. *Women in Love* (England)
   10. *Tristana* (Spain)
   11. *Kwaidan* (Japan)
   12. *Investigation of a Citizen Above Suspicion* (Italy)
   13. *Bed and Board* (France)
   14. *The Devils* (England)
   15. *Fellini Satyricon* (Italy)

   1. *The Clowns* (Italy)
   2. *Loves of a Blonde* (Czechoslovakia)
   3. *The Gladiators* (England)
   4. *The Shop on Main Street* (Czechoslovakia)
   5. *Medea* (Italy)
   6. *Macunaima* (Brazil)
   7. *War and Peace*, Part I (Russia)
   8. *War and Peace*, Part II (Russia)
   9. *Seven Samurai* (Japan)
   10. *Stolen Kisses* (France)
   11. *The End of August at the Hotel Ozone* (Czechoslovakia)
   12. *Hour of the Wolf* (Sweden)
   13. *Juliet of the Spirits* (Italy)
   14. *Rashomon* (Japan)
   15. *Performance* (England)

      b. (featuring Federico Fellini)

   1. *Fellini: A Director's Notebook* (1969)
   2. *Variety Lights* (1950)
   3. *The White Sheik* (1952)
   4. *I Vitteloni* (1953) (episode)
   5. *La Strada* (1954)

    6. *Il Bidone* (1955)
    7. *Nights of Cabiria* (1957)
    8. *La Dolce Vita* (1960)
    9. *Boccaccio '70* (1962) (episode)
  10. *8 1/2* (1963)
  11. *Juliet of the Spirits* (1965)
  12. *Spirits of the Dead* (1968) (episode)
  13. *Satyricon* (1968)
  14. *The Clowns* (1970)

c. (featuring Ingmar Bergman):

    1. *The Seventh Seal* (1956)
    2. *Wild Strawberries* (1957)
    3. *Brink of Life* (1957)
    4. *The Magician* (1958)
    5. *The Virgin Spring* (1959)
    6. *The Devil's Eye* (1960)
    7. *Through a Glass Darkly* (1961)
    8. *Winter Light* (1962)
    9. *The Silence* (1962)
  10. *Persona* (1966)
  11. *Hour of the Wolf* (1968)
  12. *Shame* (1968)
  13. *The Passion of Anna* (1969)
  14. *The Rite* (1969)
  15. *The Touch* (1970)

d. Selected director's festival:

François Truffaut
Akira Kurosawa
Gillo Pontecorvo
Costa Gavras
    1. *Battle of Algiers* (Pontecorvo)
    2. *The 400 Blows* (Truffaut)
    3. *Rashomon* (Kurosawa)
    4. *The Sleeping Car Murder* (Gavras)
    5. *Jules and Jim* (Truffaut)
    6. *Men Who Tread on the Tiger's Tail* (Kurosawa)
    7. *Z* (Gavras)
    8. *Bed and Board* (Truffaut)
    9. *Burn!* (Pontecorvo)
  10. *Seven Samurai* (Kurosawa)
  11. *The Confession* (Gavras)

12. *Mississippi Mermaid* (Truffaut)
13. *Yojimbo* (Kurosawa)
14. *Stolen Kisses* (Truffaut)
15. *The Wild Child* (Truffaut)

e. Featuring films of a particular country or countries in combination

FRANCE

1. *La Femme Infidèle*
2. *Children of Paradise*
3. *Umbrellas of Cherbourg*
4. *Weekend*
5. *The Bride Wore Black*
6. *A Man and a Woman*
7. *The Wild Child*
8. *Le Bonheur*
9. *Le Jour Se Lève*
10. *My Night at Maud's*
11. *Orpheus*
12. *Blood of a Poet* and *Un Chien Andalou*
13. *Claire's Knee*
14. *Forbidden Games*
15. *Stolen Kisses*

JAPAN

1. *Yojimbo*
2. *Tokyo Story*
3. *Seven Samurai*
4. *Ikiru*
5. *Gate of Hell*
6. *Boy*
7. *Tales of the Taira Clan*
8. *Woman in the Dunes*
9. *Men Who Tread on the Tiger's Tail*
10. *Death by Hanging*
11. *Diary of a Shinjuku Thief*
12. *Chikamatzu*
13. *Samurai*
14. *Rashomon*
15. *Kwaidan*

SWEDEN AND RUSSIA

1. *I Am Curious Yellow* (Sweden)
2. *Shame* (Sweden)

3. *Ivan the Terrible*, Part I (Russia)
4. *Ivan the Terrible*, Part II (Russia)
5. *Shadows of Forgotten Ancestors* (Russia)
6. *Ballad of a Soldier* (Sweden)
7. *My Sister, My Love* (Sweden)
8. *War and Peace*, Part I (Russia)
9. *War and Peace*, Part II (Russia)
10. *Dear John* (Sweden)
11. *The Idiot* (Russia)
12. *Aku-Aku* (Sweden)
13. *Alexander Nevsky* (Russia)
14. *Hour of the Wolf* (Sweden)
15. *The Cranes Are Flying* (Russia)

ITALY
1. *The Tenth Victim*
2. *Death in Venice*
3. *The Gospel According to St. Matthew*
4. *L'Avventura*
5. *The Conformist*
6. *Divorce—Italian Style*
7. *Seduced and Abandoned*
8. *Red Desert*
9. *8 1/2*
10. *Two Women*
11. *Boccaccio '70*
12. *General Della Rovere*
13. *The Damned*
14. *Juliet of the Spirits*
15. *Fellini Satyricon*

GREAT BRITAIN
1. *If . . .*
2. *A Taste of Honey*
3. *Darling*
4. *2001: A Space Odyssey*
5. *The Leather Boys*
6. *Far from the Madding Crowd*
7. *Morgan!*
8. *Help!*
9. *The Loneliness of the Long Distance Runner*
10. *The Collector*
11. *Ulysses*
12. *Dr. Strangelove*
13. *Marat/Sade*

14. *The Servant*
15. *The Gladiators*

CZECHOSLOVAKIA
1. *Loves of a Blonde*
2. *The Shop on Main Street*
3. *Diamonds of the Night*
4. *The Fireman's Ball*
5. *The End of August at the Hotel Ozone*
6. *Ecstasy*
7. *Good Soldier Schweik*
8. *The White Dove*
9. *The Fifth Horseman Is Fear*
10. *A Report on the Party and the Guests*

GERMANY
1. *The 1,000 Eyes of Dr. Mabuse*
2. *Triumph of the Will*
3. *The Blue Angel*
4. *The Threepenny Opera*
5. *The Cabinet of Dr. Caligari*
6. *Young Torless*
7. *Vampyr*
8. *A Taste for Love*
9. *Olympia*, Part I (1936–1938)
10. *Olympia*, Part II (1936–1938)
11. *M*
12. *Waxworks*
13. *Metropolis*
14. *Whither Germany?*
15. *Hamlet*

2. Films of "one type" festivals:
   a. Classic comedy festival
      1. *A Night at the Opera* (Marx Brothers)
      2. *My Little Chickadee* (W.C. Fields)
      3. *The Gold Rush* (Charlie Chaplin)
      4. *The General* and *Cops* (Buster Keaton)
      5. *Abbott and Costello Meet the Keystone Cops* (Abbott and Costello)
      6. *A Day at the Races* (Marx Brothers)
      7. *You Can't Cheat an Honest Man* (W.C. Fields)
      8. *Long Pants* (Harry Langdon)
      9. W.C. Fields shorts: *The Fatal Glass of Beer, The Barber*

Shop, Circus Slicker, The Great McGonigle, The Pharmacist,
The Great Train Robbery
10. *Never Give a Sucker an Even Break* (W.C. Fields)
11. Buster Keaton shorts: Your choice from seventeen silent shorts
12. Harry Langdon shorts: Your choice
13. *The Great Dictator* (Charlie Chaplin)
14. *When Comedy Was King* (compilation)
15. *The Bank Dick* (W.C. Fields)

b. Science-fiction festival:
1. *A Clockwork Orange*
2. *Fahrenheit 451*
3. *The Man with the X-Ray Eyes*
4. *Flash Gordon Conquers the Universe*
5. *The Day the Earth Stood Still*
6. *The Incredible Shrinking Man*
7. *Kronos*
8. *THX-1138*
9. *The Invasion of the Body Snatchers*
10. *2001: A Space Odyssey*
11. *Metropolis*
12. *On the Beach*
13. *The Andromeda Strain*
14. *The Time Machine*
15. *The Omega Man*
16. *Dr. Strangelove*

c. Horror film festival:
1. *Freaks*
2. *Frankenstein*
3. *The Mummy*
4. *King Kong*
5. *Kwaidan*
6. *The Horror Chamber of Dr. Faustus*
7. *Psycho*
8. *The Cabinet of Dr. Caligari*
9. *The Phantom of the Opera*
10. *Rosemary's Baby*
11. *Taste the Blood of Dracula*
12. *Wait Until Dark*
13. *The Curse of Frankenstein*
14. *Vampyr*
15. *Night of the Living Dead*

   d. Gangster film festival:
1. *Bonnie and Clyde*
2. *The Maltese Falcon*
3. *Breathless*
4. *The St. Valentine's Day Massacre*
5. *On the Waterfront*
6. *The Sicilian Clan*
7. *G-Men*
8. *Coogan's Bluff*
9. *Angels with Dirty Faces*
10. *Borsalino*
11. *M*
12. *Scarface*
13. *Never Steal Anything Small*
14. *Think Fast, Mr. Moto*
15. *Bullitt*

   e. Fifties revival festival:
1. *Rebel Without a Cause*
2. *On the Waterfront*
3. *The African Queen*
4. *The Wild One*
5. *Shock Corridor*
6. *Jailhouse Rock*
7. *I Want to Live!*
8. *Giant*
9. *Rock Around the Clock*
10. *The Young Savages*
11. *East of Eden*
12. *The Harder They Fall*
13. *On the Bowery*
14. *Rock Revival of '64*

   f. Independent film-maker's festival:
1. *Punishment Park*
2. *Hendrix at Berkeley*
3. *Dynamite Chicken*
4. *Don't Look Back*
5. *Chicago Conspiracy Circus '70*
6. *Millhouse: A White Comedy*
7. *The Last Picture Show*
8. *Easy Rider*
9. *Hellstrom Chronicle*
10. *THX-1138*
11. *Glen and Randa*

12. *Taking Off*
13. *A Face of War*
14. *Luminous Procuress* and *Tricia's Wedding*
15. *Gimme Shelter*

g. Nature and anthropological film series:
  1. *To Find Our Life: The Peyote Hunt of the Huichol Indians*
  2. *The Sky Above, the Mud Below*
  3. *Wilderness Alps of Stehekin*
  4. *The Witch Doctor, People Out of Time, Margaret Mead*
  5. *A Plague on Your Children*
  6. *Walkabout*
  7. *Why Man Creates, The Wind and the River, Take Off, Solo, Sky Capers, The Searching Eye* and *Get Wet*
  8. *Chinese Journey, Laos, Lost Men of Malaya, Spirit Mediums* and *Medico Magic*
  9. *Men of the Dream Time, Roaring Serpent of Arnhem* and *Brother of the Sun*
  10. *Kon-Tiki*
  11. *The Redwoods*
  12. *Americans of Everest, Chemical Man*
  13. *Dead Birds*
  14. *Africa, Bouquet, Deep Blue World, Divided World, Dunes, Embryo, Harvesting, Home of the Brave, Impressions of a Guatemala Market Day*
  15. *Aku-Aku*

h. Children's festival:
  1. *Alice in Wonderland* (Disney)
  2. *Swiss Family Robinson*
  3. Any Jerry Lewis film
  4. *Ichabod and Mr. Toad* (Disney)
  5. *Treasure Island*
  6. *Abbott and Costello Go to Mars*
  7. *Pinocchio*
  8. The Dead End Kids (any film)
  9. Cartoon carnival: *Mr. Magoo, Bugs Bunny, Daffy Duck, Porky Pig, Sylvester and Tweety, Betty Boop*, etc.
  10. *The Snow Queen*
  11. *Room Service* (Marx Brothers)
  12. *Alice in Wonderland* (W.C. Fields)
  13. *Destination Saturn* (Buck Rogers)
  14. *Frankenstein*
  15. *Four Clowns*

    i. Civilization film series (all available from Time/Life):
1. *The Frozen World*
2. *The Great Thaw*
3. *Romance and Reality*
4. *Man—The Measure of All Things*
5. *The Hero As Artist*
6. *Protest and Communication*
7. *Grandeur and Obedience*
8. *Light of Experience*
9. *The Pursuit of Happiness*
10. *The Smile of Reason*
11. *The Worship of Nature*
12. *The Fallacies of Hope*
13. *Heroic Materialism*

The variations in programming are endless. Specialty programs are particularly effective at locations where there are several societies in competition. A program of films from all areas might not do as well as an in-depth study of one of the areas of interest enumerated in the preceding pages.

Audience reaction to programming is important to research for future reference in booking. You might distribute a simple questionnaire to the audience as follows:

1. Did you like the film?
2. Would you like to see other films of this type?
3. Would you see this film again?
4. Any suggestions for films you would like to see?

Some distribution companies will be very happy to arrange appearances of guest speakers (film-makers, directors) at your school. Usually the companies that handle independent productions are into this. You can write to the company that handles the films of the person and find out how much he wants to be paid for speaking and how much he needs for round-trip transportation and per-diem expenses. The company will either transmit your request to the film-maker, who will then negotiate with you, or handle the arrangements directly.

DISTRIBUTORS: HOW THEY WORK

TERMS AND CONDITIONS

1. The film requested will be used only on the date and at the place indicated.

2. Films may not be loaned, rerented, donated or used in any other location without prior written consent of distributor.

3. Public advertising in any form of the exhibition of feature films— posters, radio or newspaper announcements or ads, press releases, etc.— is strictly prohibited.

4. All prints are for non-theatrical use only, and may not be used for theatrical or television purposes or in competition with regular motion-picture theaters.

5. Exhibitor will pay transportation of the film both ways.

6. Exhibitor must ship back film no later than the day following the play date via prepaid, special delivery. For each day's delay in returning the film, the exhibitor shall pay an additional charge equal to one day's rental.

7. Exhibitor shall pay cost of replacement footage for film damage caused by negligence or carelessness in use or shipping at the rate of $.15 per foot for black and white films, $.25 per foot for color films.

8. If admission is charged, exhibitor agrees to pay 50 percent of the gross receipts to distributor within seven (7) days following the play date. Minimum guarantees and flat-rental payments are to be paid in advance of the play date.

9. The exhibitor has the right to cancel any picture from this order form if such written notice is received by distributor at least ten (10) days prior to shipping date of the film.

10. Distributor reserves the right to cancel or refuse service, depending upon its approval of the use of its product.

11. *Violation of any of the restrictions of use noted above are subject to penalties set forth in Section 101 of the United States Copyright Law, carrying a liability of up to $5,000 for each violation.*

These provisions are generally the same for most distributors of 16mm films. However, condition No. 3 (publicity) is treated quite differently by a number of companies whose films are distributed mainly to film societies and small art theaters. These are the independent companies: EYR, Genesis, Newline, N.T.S., The Underground Cooperatives, Third World Cinema Group, etc. They encourage as much publicity of the screening of their films as possible, and many of them supply promotional materials expressly for this purpose. Since their selection of films is mainly independent productions that never make a theatrical run, and their primary market is the college circuit for the total exhibition of these films, they are under no pressure to limit the drawing potential of film societies.

This severe restriction on public advertising was created by the interference of theater owners, who of course are the sole supporters of the established movie industry and consequently have considerable power.

If the relationship of a society with local theater owners is good, this condition needn't be strictly adhered to.

Film rentals are the largest expense in the operation of a society. The many different companies have different ways of pricing film rentals. Generally speaking, the following holds true for most distributors:

If you show a film once, you pay the minimum rental as stated in the catalogue. For each subsequent showing, the rate is one half the base rate. If a film rents for $250 and you want to show it twice, then it will cost a minimum of $375 ($125 for the second showing). If you charge admission, then you pay this minimum guarantee versus (usually) 50 percent of the gross receipts, whichever is higher.

Some distributors will let you show the film twice on the same day for the initial minimum fee as listed in their catalogue.

Other companies will agree to multiple showings over a period of two or three days, paying the minimum rental fee in the catalogue.

In all cases, whenever admission is charged, the rental fee is the minimum guarantee as agreed upon versus 50 percent (sometimes higher) of the gross receipts, whichever is greater is the amount due the distributor.

It's best to level with distributors regarding the number of shows. By now a lot of companies realize it is to their advantage to compromise and allow groups to hold multiple exhibitions, charging the base minimum guarantee versus the percentage. By demonstrating trust in the exhibitor, they are rewarded with accurate attendance figures, prompt payment and no mishaps with their prints.

A few firms, however, refuse to bend an inch—and they must lose quite a lot in film revenues from groups that cannot afford to pay for the number of screenings they need. The saddest part is that they are denying an audience of sincere cinema appreciators (even though a small group) a film that they want very much to see.

The more business you do with a particular company, the more likelihood there is of successful bargaining. You will receive more courteous and prompt service from those who know you, as with any other business service.

Some examples of the rates charged by different companies follows:

AUDIO/BRANDON

Rental Rates

Rental rates are based on TYPE of showing and CLASSIFICATION of the film except those films for which a rental is already indicated in the catalogue.

Type 1

No admission charge, subscription fee or collection. Attendance *not exceeding* 250 people.

Type 2

No admission charge, subscription fee or collection. Attendance *over* 250 people.

Type 3

Admission or subscription fee charged or collection taken, attendance *not exceeding* 250 people.

Type 4

Admission or subscription fee charged or collection taken, attendance *over* 250 people.

After determining type of showing, check table below for rental rate of films you select according to classifications A thru F.

Type	A	B	C	D	E	F
1	$30.00	$40.00	$55.00	$65.00	$75.00	$110.00
2	35.00	45.00	60.00	75.00	100.00	135.00
3	40.00	55.00	75.00	100.00	125.00	175.00
4	45.00	65.00	*100.00	*125.00	*150.00	*200.00

* Minimum guarantee against (50%) of gross receipts, whichever is higher.

SAVE $15.00 BY BOOKING SIX FEATURES AT ONE TIME! A discount of $2.50 per feature is given when six (6) or more features are booked at one time for showing during one year.

(Their least popular are Type A; their best renting titles are Type F.)

Rental Rates

All rental rates indicated are for a one day rental only. The rental rate for two or three days' use is the one day rate plus 50% (except Walt Disney films); the rental rate for four to seven days' use is twice the one day rental (except Walt Disney films). Special rates that apply for multiple day bookings on Walt Disney films will be supplied on request. A series discount of $2.50 per feature will be allowed when six or more features are booked at one time for showing during one year (except on Walt Disney films).

JANUS FILMS

16MM INFORMATION FOR NON-COMMERCIAL EXHIBITION

Price

The following prices are applicable to all individual films in the Janus catalogue.

	Base Rate		Discount* Rate	
Type of Showing	*B & W*	*Color*	*B & W*	*Color*
Janus Standard Collection	$120	$150	$96*	$120*
Janus British Collection	80	100	64*	80*
Special Religious Rates: Churches, Synagogues, YM&YWCA's & YM&YWHA's and Other Religious Organizations	80	100	64*	80*
Special High School Rates	75	90	60*	72*

* Multi-order Discount: Save 20% on each film by ordering any six (6) films in the Janus catalogue to be played off within one year.

Additional Showings

Rental rates listed are for one showing. For two or more showings on the same day or on two consecutive days, at the same location, the rental is one-and-a-half times the base rate.

Box Office Report

Box office report must be returned on all showings where attendance is over 200.

When admission is charged the price is always the base rate vs. 50 percent of the gross receipts, or when no admission fee is charged there is an additional charge of $.25 for each person above 300 in attendance.

Please apply for rental quotation where attendance will exceed 500, giving size of hall and full particulars.

FILMS, INC.

Sliding Scale of Rental Rates

These rental rates are based on a sliding scale according to the *Type* of showing and the *Classification* of the film, except those films which have a Minimum Rental (M) price in the current listing. Minimum Rental prices apply except where the sliding scale rates are higher.

These rates are for one showing only. The rate for two showings on the same day or on consecutive days, at the same location, is one-and-a-half (1-1/2) times the rate for one showing. Transportation and handling charges are additional.

When admission is charged, whether by subscription fee, membership dues or collection, and the audience size exceeds 200, rentals shown are minimum guarantees against a percentage of the gross receipts at a rate to be negotiated with your local exchange—whichever amount is larger.

NOTE: Prisons, hospitals and other bona-fide shut-ins are entitled to special rental rates. Write to your nearest exchange for non-theatrical showings and rates.

Types 1 through 5: rates especially designed for schools and convents where no admission is charged*—not open to the general public.

Type	Audience Size	*	* *	* * *	Special
1	less than 100	$15.00	$25.00	$30.00	$50.00
2	101-250	25.00	30.00	40.00	75.00
3	251-500	30.00	35.00	45.00	100.00
4	501-1000	35.00	40.00	65.00	125.00
5	over 1000	45.00	50.00	75.00	150.00

Types 6 to 12: rates apply to colleges, universities, museums, and film society showings where no admission is charged*—not open to the general public. A Standard License Agreement obtained through Films Incorporated must be completed and returned, prior to any showing. Violation of this agreement will revoke your location approval.

Type	Audience Size	*	* *	* * *	Special
6	less than 100	$30.00	$35.00	$45.00	$65.00
7	101-250	40.00	45.00	65.00	100.00
8	251-500	50.00	60.00	85.00	125.00
9	501-750	55.00	65.00	95.00	150.00
10	751-1000	75.00	85.00	120.00	190.00
11	1001-1250	90.00	100.00	140.00	225.00
12	over 1251	100.00	115.00	170.00	250.00

Their least popular films are rated *, their most popular "special."

CONTEMPORARY FILMS

Feature Rental Rates

Rental rates of feature films are based on type of audience (restricted, unrestricted, admission charged) and classification of films as indicated (B, C, S, E), except for those films for which a flat rental fee is shown. There is, in addition, a nominal shipping charge. Feature film rentals apply for one showing only.

(Apply for rates for more than one screening. Their least popular are rated B; most popular are rated E.)

A 15% discount will be applied against the basic rental when five or more FEATURE FILMS are ordered at one time.

Restricted: (no admission charge)	Members of a class, club or study group where there is no public announcement.
Unrestricted: (no admission charge)	Any showing announced to the campus or public.
Admission Charged:	Any showing with admission charge, subscription fee, collection, dues, or any other form of payment.

	B	C	S	E
Restricted (no admission charge)	$35	$50	$ 60	$ 75
Unrestricted (no admission charge)	50	75	100	125
Admission Charged	50*	75*	100*	125*

* Price indicated is a minimum guarantee against 50% of the gross receipts to be reported within 24 hours after the showing.

These rental rates apply to 16mm. prints only.

Films that are available in 35mm. are indicated throughout the catalogue. For information regarding the rental of 35mm. prints, write to: PATHE CONTEMPORARY FILMS/McGRAW-HILL, 330 West 42nd Street, New York, N.Y. 10036.

WARNER BROTHERS

No types or classifications of exhibitors or circumstances is provided for. Each film has its own minimum rental fee; prices vary from $150 to $750.

Multiple Exhibitions

Listed rental rates are for *one exhibition only.* Where multiple showings are planned the first exhibition shall be at the listed rate and each of the subsequent exhibitions shall be at 50 percent of the listed rate.

When Admission Is Charged

The basic rental rate becomes a guarantee versus 50 percent of the gross receipts (whichever is greater) when admission is charged. Warner Bros., Inc. will, at time of print shipment, forward to you under separate cover an Income Participation Report. All requested information must be supplied, and the report must be returned within twenty-four hours after playdate.

UNIVERSAL/16

Rental Rates for College,
Universities, Museums and Film Societies

Rental rates listed in this index apply to two showings of each film in a single location on one day. If admission is charged, the rates listed becomes the minimum guarantee vs. 50 percent of the gross receipts, whichever is greater. Each film has its own base rental. They have rates for general recreation; and rates for church groups and shut-ins may be applied for.

COLUMBIA CINEMATHEQUE

Rentals are for one showing only. Where admission is charged, rental price acts as guarantee vs. 50 percent of gross receipts (whichever is larger). All rental payments are due seven days in advance of shipping dates; where admission is charged, a head count must be submitted immediately following the play date, and where there are overages you will be billed subsequently.

Each film has its own base rental. Multiple screenings: Apply.

UA/16 FILM LIBRARY

Each film has its own rental rate ($100–$200 minimum).

Rental: All rentals are for one (1) showing in one (1) location on one (1) day only.

If admission is charged, you pay prices quoted as minimum guarantee or 50 percent of the gross receipts, whichever is larger.

Multiple screenings: 1/2 the base rate for each additional showing.

UA/16 FILM LIBRARY "GOLDEN TREASURY" CATALOGUE

All black and white feature motion pictures in this 16mm catalogue are priced at $50. All feature motion pictures in color are priced at $75. (Color features in this catalogue are not available in black and white.)

Each Newsreel Program is priced at $15.

Short Subjects are priced as follows: $10 for one-reel subjects, $15 for two-reel subjects.

All cartoons are priced at $10 each.

All rentals are for one (1) showing in one (1) location on one (1) day only.

When admission is charged for feature films, you pay prices quoted as a minimum guarantee or 50 percent of the gross receipts, whichever is higher.

Multiple screenings: 1/2 the base rate for each subsequent showing.

EYR CAMPUS PROGRAMS

Feature Film Non-Theatrical Rentals

	Admission	No Admission
1 film	$175 vs. 65%	$150
4 films	$150 vs. 65% each	$125 each
7 films	$125 vs. 65% each	$100 each

Multiple screenings: Apply. (Lenient Dist.)

NEW YORKER FILMS—FEATURE RENTAL RATES

Rental rates of feature films are based on type of audience (restricted, unrestricted, admission charged) and classification of films as indicated in catalogue (B, C, S, E).

Restricted:

Members of a class, club or study group where there is no public announcement.

Unrestricted:

Any showing announced to the campus or public.

Admission Charged:

Any showing with admission charge, subscription fee, collection, dues, or any other form of payment.

	B	*C*	*S*	*E*
Restricted	$35	$50	$60	$75
Unrestricted	50	75	100	125
Admission Charged	50*	75*	100*	125*

* Prince indicated is a minimum guarantee against 50% of the gross receipts to be reported within 24 hours after the showing.

A discount of $5 per feature is given when six (6) or more features are booked at one time for showing during one twelve-month period.

Agreement:

1) Film rental is for one showing only at the specified address.
2) Customers are responsible and will be billed for extensive damage resulting from careless handling.
3) Films are not to be shown on television or duplicated without written clearance from New Yorker Films.

Please Note:

Motion pictures are copyrighted and are licensed for exhibition only at the time and place specified. Any exhibition other than at the time and place specified is a violation of Section 101 of the U.S. Copyright laws and carries penalties up to $5,000 for each violation.

Multiple screenings: Apply.

WALTER READE 16

General Rental Rates and Payment

The rates on the Walter Reade 16 Price Index are for one showing at one location on one date. To avoid extra-day charges, films must be returned not later than the day following the showing. The charge for retaining a film longer than one day is fifty percent (50%) of initial rental per day, discounted or otherwise. It is understood that the authorized representative will certify the following:

1. No admission, collection, or subscription is charged.
2. The group does not exceed one hundred-twenty-five (125) persons.
3. The film is shown one time on one date at one location.
4. Payment must be made upon receipt of our invoice.

For additional showings or rental periods, inquire for rates. To obtain classroom rates, write or call.

Certain titles are available on an annual lease basis.

Rates for Paid Performances

When admission, collection, or subscription is charged, you pay the prices quoted in the Price Index as a minimum guarantee or fifty percent (50%) of the gross receipts, whichever is larger. A complete box office report must be submitted to Walter Reade 16 immediately upon the completion of the showing. Indicating the number in attendance and the total amount of paid admissions to each performance, together with a check for the balance due.

Each film has its own base rental. Multiple screenings: Apply.

NEWLINE CINEMA

Apply for rates. This company is one of those with whom it is a delight to work. They will generally discuss the rental fee with you before deciding what it should be according to what you think you can do with a film. They have no rules about so much for one extra exhibition, etc. (generally 50 percent of gross receipts).

GENESIS FILMS

Apply for rates. They also are very easy to work with. No hard-and-fast rules about extra exhibition rental fees. Generally 50 percent of gross receipts.

SWANK MOTION PICTURES

Each film has its own base rental. Generally the fee for multiple exhibitions is one-half the base rate for each extra screening. However, the company is quite willing to work with exhibitors on this, so they *can* afford to rent high-priced films and show them a number of times for a fixed guarantee vs. 50 percent of gross receipts.

ALL COMPANIES CARRY THE FOLLOWING RULE

License

All films are copyrighted and are licensed for exhibition only at the time and place specified by contract. Any other exhibition or use of the film is a violation of Section 101 of the U.S. copyright laws and carries penalties up to $5,000 for each violation. Rentals are subject to the condition that the film will not be altered, televised, reproduced or transmitted in any form or by any means, electronic or mechanical, including photocopy, recording, or any information storage and retrieval system now known or to be invented.

In defense of distributors, the following should be thought about before you scream rip-off.

WHAT A FILM RENTAL COST REFLECTS

1. *Original print acquisition:*
    a. Financial arrangements for the right to distribute the film to the 16mm non-theatrical market.
    b. Either buying prints or having new ones made. (Many prints of each title must be maintained by each distributor that offers it for rent.)
2. Maintenance of prints—inspecting, shipping and receiving. Doctoring scratches, replacing ruined footage of the films and the head and tail leaders, etc.
3. *Bookings per print* cannot of necessity be too frequent or the company would foul up delivering prints on time. This means that each print of a film has a potential maximum use of only three times per month.
4. *Miscellaneous*—all other regular office expenses, including their promotional campaign to reach clients.

Some companies are really too high-priced; others may seem to be, but after you've had a few months' experience the old adage of "you get what you pay for" might ring true. Others are downright bargains and provide good service also. All too soon you'll find out who are the most difficult to work with, regardless of what they charge.

Remember that you can always bargain with a distributor. You might find, to your pleasant surprise, that a film you previously thought was out of your rental range can be secured at a lower fee. Sometimes also, if you wait six months to a year, the fee will be reduced. This is true usually for new releases that command very high prices in the 16mm market directly after their theatrical run. The demand for these films decreases after they have been out to the non-theatrical market for a while, and at that time there is a good chance of obtaining them at lower fees.

BOOKING THE FILM

After the program has been picked, the chairman and secretary should get together for as long as it takes to write all the distributors of the different films.

SAMPLE LETTER

——————————
——————————
——————————

Gentlemen:

We are interested in renting the following titles on the following date(s):

| | (1st choice) | (alternate play date) |
Title	Date	Date
———————	———————	———————
Title	Date	Date
———————	———————	———————

1. Number of days each film to be shown _____
2. Number of performances for each film _____
3. Seating capacity _____ Name of auditorium _____
4. Admission _____

5. Name and phone number of person in charge _____

6. Ship via (airmail, parcel post, air freight, etc.) _____

7. Shipping address: Billing address:

_____   _____

_____   _____

_____   _____

Please send samples of publicity materials available for these films, including reviews, stills, press books, program notes, handbills or posters. When confirming, please advise what the minimum guarantee rental for each film will be.

Sincerely,

_____

_____

With a letter such as this, the distributor is furnished with all the information he needs to respond to your request quickly. Hopefully but not assuredly. Sometimes getting confirmation takes forever for no apparent reason other than bureaucratic paper shuffling.

After these initial letters have gone out, wait ten working days for confirmations. You should be most concerned with replies to your first-half program. If you haven't heard about these seven or eight films after ten working days, write again, this time *special delivery*, with the note SECOND REQUEST on the top of the letter in *red*.

What you want from the distributor is a written contract or invoice, complete with shipping date, shipping information, rental fee and play dates listed clearly. You should *check carefully* the *shipping address* and note by what date the advance payment is due and by what *method* the film is being sent to you.

If time is growing short and you have still not heard from the distributors of the first four films, you should call them collect. Some firms will accept the charges collect; others will not. If the oversight in booking is theirs, you should feel free to deduct the cost of the call from the rental fee. Even if you lock horns and the company adamantly insists you pay for the call, remember that the information, good or bad, gained by spending ten dollars or so on a phone call is well worth it.

Keeping all correspondence and rental contracts is essential. In addition, you might want to draw up a master checklist as follows:

Date request first mailed: _____   * Film

Film Title: _____   * confirmed for

Distributor: Name   *
            Address   _____
            Phone number
            Personal contact

Show date requested: 1st choice _____ alternate _____

Second request mailed _____

Telephone call placed _____ (indicate charges)

Rental fee: $_____

Payment in advance: (yes) _____ (no) _____

Date check must reach distributor _____ (before ship date)

Shipping date: _____ via: _____

In this fashion you need not leaf through piles of correspondence each time the status of the schedule must be checked, to learn what needs to be done to solidify the season. It's all on one card.

Again, the need to book as far in advance as possible cannot be over-stressed. There is a terrific demand for new-release films, and often older films that are still quite popular are booked months in advance.

Try to maintain pleasant working relations with distributors. If you must cancel a film, give as much notice as possible. Pay your bills promptly. Ship the films back the day after showing.

If requested not to rewind the prints, leave them tails out. Many companies completely inspect and clean each print after each rental. It's far easier for them if the print is returned not rewound.

When shipping, the print should be insured for a minimum of $200 per feature, $50 per short.

Whenever you have damaged a film while in your possession, let the distributor know about it. The damage could escape his attention, and the next film society unlucky enough to get that particular print will have to cope with the print. It could happen to you.

The better organized you are, the easier it will be for you. Once all the mechanics are set in motion you will know when your films are expected to arrive, how they are being shipped and whether or not you need to pay for them in advance to *insure* their being shipped. Your promotional materials will arrive when you can make the best use of them, not on the day of the film.

SHIPPING, RECEIVING AND DELAYED PRINTS

Of course, films do get delayed. In my four years of experience it has happened to our group about five times for various reasons. The most common was the distributor sending the film using the U.S. postal system and either not marking the film *airmail* clearly enough or sending it surface mail, fourth-class rate from New York to Honolulu! If you are in close proximity to the company, this doesn't matter; there's no problem. I prefer to receive films by air freight and return them by airmail special delivery, insured for the maximum of $200. Never has a film I returned by this method been lost, so it must be assumed it is not the postal authorities who are at fault but the shipping clerks who don't mark *airmail* or *special delivery* clearly enough. And around Christmastime an extra week should be allowed for receipt of films. Air freight can be delayed also, but at least there is a way to determine the location of the shipment if you know which air freight company or freight forwarder is handling the film. Airmail is faster and cheaper when it's marked clearly. Air freight is almost twice as expensive, but far fewer chances of mishaps are involved when you receive prints this way.

If you are within a couple of hundred mile radius of the distributor, it is safe to receive and send your films via *special fourth-class rate*, 16mm films, parcel-post special delivery, insured for $200, provided the distributor will mail the film ten working days in advance of play date.

If there is *air freight service* between you and the distributor, fine. Have the distributor send the film seven days in advance of play date.

Should you choose *airmail special delivery*, allow ten working days for receipt.

If your show is scheduled for Friday and you haven't received the film by Wednesday morning, it's time to act,

1. Recheck the confirmation or invoice form sent to you by the distributor. Perhaps you have mistaken the method of shipment and are running to the post office when all along the film has been waiting for you at an air-freight terminal.

You could be calling the wrong air-freight company.

Perhaps the shipping address is wrong, an error which should have been caught when the confirmation was first received; but if noticed only now, perhaps the film can be located.

Maybe the distributor scheduled prints of this film very tightly and shipped it only Tuesday, destined to arrive Thursday, or the day of your show, Friday. I would call him to find out.

2. If you cannot locate the film, or have reason to believe it will not

arrive on time, call the distributor and find out 1) when it was shipped; 2) by what method.

If it was sent seven to ten days in advance by the postal system, assume it will not arrive on time. *Demand a replacement print.*

If it was sent seven to ten days in advance by an air-freight company, verify which company and find out the airway bill number. Have the distributor trace the shipment from his end, and you also send a tracer from your side. If the film can't be located, *demand a replacement print.*

3. If the distributor doesn't have another print of that film on hand, you are out of luck. You must book a substitute film. As long as you've got them on the phone you might try for one of their films. If not, hopefully you have compiled a listing of local sources where a film can be obtained at short notice. This is where keeping your list of alternates decided upon when the program was originally selected comes in handy. You must act quickly, and there simply isn't time to figure out *what* film to show.

Substituting a different film than what was advertised and expected by your patrons is disappointing to them, yes, but much preferable to their arriving at a darkened, empty, lifeless auditorium with a hand-lettered *No Show—Film Canceled* sign on the door. The people will appreciate your ability to provide an alternate film for them. Once they're out and have come all the way there, they will probably stay. Even if they don't, you have at least done your best to avoid disappointing the crowd—a fact they will appreciate and remember.

SUMMARY

Find out what films people *want* to see. A schedule of perfectly good films can be chosen, but if they are of interest only to a few individuals, the society is destined to failure. This may mean running films that are not particularly outstanding except as general entertainment, but don't belittle these titles, as they will provide the extra funds necessary to book less popular, more "worthwhile" films; and, besides, it's not dishonorable to provide entertainment. You don't want to crush your audience with too heavy a program.

Do book well in advance. Secure definite confirmations. Either a contract or an invoice will do, complete with rental fee clearly listed.

Keep well up to date on new releases. The research committee should constantly be at the task of updating catalogues and reviewing film periodicals.

Picking a successful program is the one area of film-society operation that can't wait for experience. It's got to be right from the outset, so be very confident that the program selected contains the right choices.

NON-ADMISSION-CHARGING GROUPS

This book is concerned mainly with information and advice pertaining to groups who must charge admission for film screening, or charter paying subscribing members for support.

Here our attention will be focused on organizations and institutions that show films as an addition to an enhancement of their general program and do not charge admission.

Briefly, the listing of places would be:

1. Grade and high schools (both classroom use and assembly or free-time entertainment).
2. Private and parochial schools (both classroom use and assembly or free-time entertainment).
3. Colleges and universities (classroom use).
4. Hospitals and sanitaria and some military bases and prisons (both entertainment and instructional uses).
5. Museums (entertaining educational films).
6. Community-service groups (entertainment, instructional and educational films).
7. Youth clubs and groups (entertainment and instructional films).
8. Children's summer camps (nature, instructional and entertainment films).
9. Churches and synagogues (for the children—entertainment, perhaps also instructional; for the adults—instructional, educational, documentaries, travelogues and entertainment).
10. Private homes (educational and entertainment films).

As all these groups do not generally charge admission, they are sometimes entitled to much lower rental fees than groups that do. However, if ever the films are shown to large audiences (250 to 500 and up), distributors do tend to raise the price according to the expected turnout, even though no admission is being charged.

CLASSROOM SHOWINGS

Films for this purpose can generally be arranged for at *minimum* prices, meaning the lowest price available on a certain film, since it is being screened to under 100 persons, with no admission being charged. Most distributors require an official, signed purchase order from the school's bookkeeping department before they will send the film.

ASSEMBLY-HALL ENTERTAINMENT

The rates for this type of screening are determined by the size of the audience. Distributors will often request the seating capacity of a particular auditorium, using this figure as the basis of their rental computations. They will also ask you how many people you expect to attend and the enrollment of the school. As with classroom showings, a signed official purchase order is necessary to receive confirmation of title(s) requested.

HOSPITALS, SANITARIA, PRISONS AND
SOME MILITARY BASES

Whenever dealing with a bona-fide shut-in—meaning that the prospective audience cannot leave that place and has access to no entertainment (movies or otherwise) other than what is provided for them there—distribution companies generally allow very low rates.

When writing distributors tell them the following: What your overall budget is for the fiscal year for supplying films to the inmates; how many films you hope to be able to bring in for this amount of money; how many people will be seeing the film; and the total population of the institution. In this way they may be more willing to lower rental fees substantially, for they will see that by charging the regular rate you won't be able to have an adequate program (if this is the case, that you have a small budget to work with). Working with one company in particular for all the films you want is a good idea. As long as they are being given your entire budget, they will do the best they can to help you out.

MUSEUMS

Art, dance, history and nature films to begin with usually have a reasonable rental fee. Here also, working with one distributor—telling him your budget, etc.—can sometimes enable you to show more films than you previously thought possible according to the amount of money you have.

COMMUNITY SERVICE AND YOUTH GROUPS

These groups generally show films for a culturally deprived section of the community—for people who need to be motivated, included in activities, taught revolutionary concepts or introduced to new ideas. Nature films, political films, instructional films, entertaining films with moral lessons—all these types of cinema are available, the rental fees again usually set low to make an adequate program possible.

CHILDREN'S SUMMER CAMPS

Unless the camp is way out in the sticks, the shut-in rates don't apply, for oftentimes there is a local commercial theater in the small town nearby that needs the business and would protest vehemently if the camps were able to rent films for almost nothing. Here again, the rental fee is determined by the number of persons attending the screening, arrived at by the size (number of seats) of the screening facility and the enrollment of the camp.

CHURCHES AND SYNAGOGUES

Apply for rates. Work with one distributor and tell him your budget.

PRIVATE HOMES

Usually very cheap.

In all cases where it is advised to work with one distributor, it should be noted that shopping around for the best deal will help find the company that it is most agreeable to do business with. Also check your catalogues first to see that you don't end up paying what a regular film society pays! You can write a letter along the following general lines:

_____

_____

_____

Gentlemen:

We are thinking of putting on a film program at our institution, whose enrollment is _____. We would expect $\underline{\text{(minimum)}}$ to $\underline{\text{(maximum)}}$ persons to attend. The seating capacity of the room we are planning to use for this purpose is _____. No admission will be charged. The budget that has been allocated for this purpose for the fiscal year is _____. We would like to be able to show a new film (every day, twice a week, once a week, bimonthly, monthly). Each film will be screened $\underline{\text{(number of performances)}}$ times.

The titles and dates we are interested in are:

_____   _____
_____   _____
_____   _____
_____   _____

We would very much appreciate any considerations you could give us concerning rental fees, as we want to supply as much entertainment (instruction, education, etc.) as possible for the amount of money we have.

We look forward to hearing from you.

Very truly yours,

_____

_____

When the replies come in you can get the catalogues out for each company and determine who is giving you the best break. Work with the company that offers you the best prices.

The following periodicals should prove especially helpful to educators and librarians:

AFI Education Membership Newsletter
American Film Institute
1815 H Street, N.W.
Washington, D.C.   20006

Audiovisual Instruction
AECT
1201—16th Street, N.W.
Washington, D.C. 20036

Film Library Quarterly
Film Library Information
Council
17 W. 60th Street
New York   10023

Film News
250 W. 57th Street
New York   10019

Media and Methods
134 N. 13th Street
Philadelphia   19107

Modern Media Teacher—
Also "See" (Screen Educators Society)
George A. Pflaum
Dayton, Ohio

Sightlines
17 W. 60th Street
New York 10023

5

Publicity

HOW TO DESIGN PROMOTIONS

When a group is first beginning it is easier to handle the advertising show by show. Rather than attempting the task of printing an elaborate program for the season, a weekly announcement will do for the first few shows, or until you are ready to begin promoting subscription memberships.

The weekly announcement can be as simple or as elaborate as you like, depending on many different factors, the first of which is your competition. If you are advertising a film on a campus or in the community where there is an abundance of movie entertainment, you should strive to make the handbill as special and distinctive as possible within your budget allowance. Generally speaking, it is not outrageous to allot 25 percent of the club's entire budget for publicity (handbills, hired help, paid advertisements). Conversely, if there's no competition, a simple typewritten announcement run off on a ditto machine might well be all that is needed to secure the expected turnout. Midway between these two is the flyer, which is prepared from black-and-white originals, pasted up on a 8-1/2 x 11 or 8-1/2 x 14 piece of paper and duplicated by the photo-offset process. This flyer can be used as a poster and also as a handbill. Photo-offset is cheap. You can make a very attractive flyer with it, and there's usually one printer using this method of duplicating to be found in every town large enough to support a film group. If there isn't one in town, Postal Instant Press has over 150 offices nationwide and in Canada. You can write Mr. Bill Levine, Postal Instant Press, P.O. Box 35155, Los Angeles, California 90035 and ask for a price list, or the branch office nearest you. Then you can mail that branch your original and a check for the advance payment plus return postage. Allow two weeks for delivery.

Remember that you don't have to be an artist to design an effective, appealing movie announcement.

The following information should be included, listed in order of importance:

1. *Title of film.* Keep it relatively large, clear and distinct.
2. *Director.* If he's not well known, this can be small; but if he is famous, large lettering is in order.
3. *Good visual image.* A picture of the actors in a dynamic or intriguing pose is preferred. The professional advertising that accompanied the film when first released can also be used effectively.
4. *Actors and actresses.* If very famous, list distinctly large
5. *Awards* won; *festivals* at which the film has been exhibited.
6. *Reviews.* If they are raves, this could be more important than any other element enumerated in this list.
7. *Capsule story plot.* Don't tell the ending.
8. If the film screenplay was adapted from a well-known piece of writing, this should be indicated, as well as the author.
9. Date, time, place, admission charge.
10. Color or black-and-white, running time, country of production, English language, subtitled or dubbed, year of production.
11. Organization sponsoring event. Phone number for information.

GATHERING THESE MATERIALS

Almost all catalogues have at least one small picture for each film as well as reviews and the story plot. Some distributors have come to realize that supplying good promotionals is the best way to secure clients. The easier they can make it for you to advertise their film, the more likely it is you will want to show it. As a result, some companies have designed promotional kits to accompany their films. EYR, Genesis and Newline Cinema have the best promotional packets for the college market, in addition to having some of the best films. From them you can obtain 8 x 10 glossy black-and-white stills, large posters and flyers. Some will include these in the price of the rental; others will charge extra but certainly less than a group would pay to have it done themselves. Newline supplies "coming attraction" trailers for most of their films, as does Genesis Films. EYR supplies the trailers and also precut radio spots.

Oftentimes other companies will make available 8 x 10 black-and-white glossies, sheets of reviews or possibly press books. Press books provide the easiest and cleanest copy to work from. They are designed by the major studios when the films are first released theatrically and are designed so the theaters can simply cut out what they want to use for newspaper ads, easy reproduction being their chief feature. They are large (11 x 17 approximately), four to five pages long and contain all the possible advertising anyone could want for any particular title, in every size and shape conceivably needed. The best feature of press books, from a printing point of view, is that all the photographs are already "screened" (broken down into tiny dots, really, like comic-book pictures) and can easily be reproduced via photo-offset with excellent results. When you are dealing with black-and-white glossy or color originals, these must be first taken to a graphics shop to be "screened" before they can be reproduced by photo-offset. Your printer can handle this, or direct you to a graphics company that will do the work.

If the distribution company cannot supply you with press books for their films, you can try writing to:

Donald L. Velde, Inc.
311 West 43rd Street
New York 10036

Velde has the largest assortment of theatrical posters, 8 x 10 black-and-white glossies and press books that are currently available from one source for 16mm films.

Sometimes it is impossible to obtain any advertising whatsoever for a given film through the distributor or Velde and you haven't been involved with the club long enough to have accumulated film periodicals and newspapers that are excellent sources. What then do you do? There's a handy device known as the *Reader's Guide to Periodical Literature*, where, under the entry "motion pictures," all the publications that have carried reviews on a particular title are listed, as well as notations as to which of these have a photograph for the film. This index is at your library, and all you need to know is the approximate date the film was theatrically released, as the volumes are compiled *chronologically* and then refer to the periodical to check it out. Reviews for a film are often spread out over a period of a year, so check thoroughly before giving up. Whether or not all the periodicals referred to in the guide are at your library is another story. However if you are fortunate, the periodical *will* be there, and it *will* have a photo and a review. If you secure the good graces of the librarian, you may be able to borrow the periodical that has an adequate photo, review, etc., and have it copied by photo-offset at the printer. One or two copies is all you need for paste-up. Never try to Xerox a picture. It won't come out well enough to be reproduced via photo-offset. You can, however, Xerox written copy, as it will reproduce well enough at least to be legible. If the periodical is not at your library, perhaps there is a used bookstore nearby that carries out-of-date magazines.

The following periodicals are a good source of advertising, although it may take over a year of subscribing to any one of them before you will be able to utilize the reviews, pictures and ads contained therein. In any event, keeping abreast of new titles and distributors is essential, so reading and saving these publications will serve a double purpose:

Film Society Review	*San Francisco Chronicle* (Sundays only)
Film Quarterly	*Rolling Stone*
Film Comment	*Inter/View*
The Village Voice	*New York Times* (Sundays only)

MAKING THE FLYER

Gather together all the information you've been able to collect. Probably you will have:

ELVIRA MADIGAN

1) A Picture:

2) A Review:

> *"Exquisite is the only word that surges in my mind as an appropriate description of this exceptional film. Its color is absolutely gorgeous. The use of music and, equally eloquent, of silences and sounds is beyond verbal description. The performers are perfect —that is the only word"*
>
> BOSLEY CROWTHER
> — *The New York Times*

You will know:

1. The director is Bo Widerberg
2. Stars are Pia Degermark, Thommy Berggren
3. 1967 Cannes Festival Best Actress: Pia Degermark
4. It is a love story
5. Country of production: Sweden
   Year of production: 1966
   Color
   90 minutes
   English subtitled
6. Your date, time, place, admission charge, your organization's name and a phone number for further information.

Since you want to make the poster look as nice as possible—attractive, clean and uncluttered, *legible*—it is best to avoid hand-lettering all the information that you can't readily cut out of a catalogue or a review for paste-up.

Dry-transfer letters that can be purchased at every stationery store are a very easy means of neatly putting all this information on the paper original. These letters come on plastic sheets. You rub them off onto the paper with a pencil point, the blunter the better. They come in every style—print, script, fancy and plain—and every size from the tiniest print imaginable to letters a full two inches tall.

The title can be something like this:

The award like so:

1967 CANNES FESTIVAL
—Best Actress—
PIA DEGERMARK

(from catalogue):

Use whatever you can from the catalogue to avoid wasting energy of transferring letters and so on until you wind up with a flyer something like this:

The border helps to make the poster more defined—more likely to attract the eye than it would be without it. Borders are available in dry-transfer letter, or you can find them in magazines or cut from calendars.

Wherever possible, use whatever typeset copy you have available, unless it is too small to be effective. For instance, very rarely do catalogues include a title that is in letters large enough to be usable. These you must almost always make.

Now, *Elvira Madigan* is a well-known film, with a very good reputation, so already there is an advantage. What about a film that hasn't been released theatrically? No one has heard of it, but you do have reviews and a picture. How do you go about imparting the feeling that this is a "must see" film?

If the reviews are good, you're set. If you also have a good promotional photo to work with, so much the better. I would feature the reviews first, the photo next and the title third, in order of importance. Of course if the director is well known or one of the actors has earned some fame, you'll want to play that up also. Juggle the elements. If you have chosen the film there must be something special about it that made you pick it. Probably the reason you picked it is the same reason other people will want to see it. Always ask yourself when making a flyer, "Why would I be motivated to see this film?" (Note illustration *Hallucinations*—a program composed of short films.)

Include as much information about the film as you have readily available. People like to know what to expect when they're thinking of going to the movies, what the critics thought of the film, etc.

Some photo-offset printers offer ink colors other than black. Most shops at least have different colored paper. Paper comes in different weights. Index-card weight is sometimes nice to use—more substantial than regular twenty-pound-weight paper. A slight difference, but it is different. Try to utilize different color compositions as much as possible. Likewise, try to vary your layout from time to time. You may find yourself comfortable with a certain pattern, but try not to have the posters all looking alike from week to week. Even changing from horizontal to vertical on an 8-1/2 x 11 piece of paper can make the poster unique from the one that preceded it. Remember that the object is first to catch the eye and then to hold the person's attention once he has noticed the flyer.

Paper can be cut various ways to achieve eye-catching results:

HALLUCINATIONS

AND OTHER FILMS

6 MIN. HALLUCINATIONS

These are twelve erotic, subconscious tableaux envisioned in the twilight between waking and sleeping. Nudes and semi-abstract shapes in bizarre surrealistic compositions produce a macabre atmosphere of dreams enhanced by *musique concrete*. *Edinburgh International Film Festival presentation; Arets Smallfilm Award, Stockholm.*

7 MIN. THE MECHANICS OF LOVE

Assistant Director: Ben Moore.

A symbolic interpretation of lovemaking, with original zither score by John Gruen. "Daring and ingenious . . . daring because of its 'forbidden' subject matter; ingenious because commonplace objects are uncommonly related to build an action without actors, the effect of which is vivid, witty, and downright bold."—Lewis Jacobs.

MECHANICS OF LOVE

15 MIN. MONKEY INTO MAN

Julian Huxley's classic study of ape behavior, a prevocative, amusing, and beautifully produced comment on evolution. "A masterpiece, worth a trip anytime, any distance . . . a film no educated person would want to miss. If Cinema 16 can find more like it, its success will be sensational."—Archer Winsten, *The New York Post.*

10 MIN. COLOR THE BIG "O" AND OTHER FILMS

Imaginative visual variations on the letter "O" in the form of an animated doodle. On the same reel: THE ROOM: " . . . first shown in its naked decay; gradually the walls are traced over by an invisible, maniacal hand, which covers every inch with small colorful designs."—Dore Ashton, *The New York Times*; and THE WEAVERS: a growing, decorative canvas, influenced by Indian art. D'Avino's decorative style and lively sense of humor have won this New York painter several Creative Film Foundation Awards for his animated films.

12 MIN. REFLECTIONS ON BLACK

Four possible sexual dreams visualized by a blind man. A highly original experiment, accompanied by a startling sound track. *Award of Distinction, Creative Film Foundation.*

10 MIN. PSYCHOMONTAGE

The Kronhausens are best known for their literary and psychological research into matters sexual, having written two books, *Pornography and the Law*, and *The Sexually Responsive Woman*. Drawing from their vast store of knowledge within their field for the execution of PSYCHOMONTAGE, the Kronhausens have allowed their creative imaginations full swing.

PSYCHOMONTAGE is a witty and at times shocking discovery of sexuality in humans and in the animal world. The Kronhausens utilize visual puns and startling symbolic juxtapositions to further their effects.

The Kronhausens treat nudity and sexual involvement with an unabashed good humor and honesty. Traditionally opposed to any form of censorship, the couple has extended their exploration of sex to a visual media and through PSYCHOMONTAGE they have exposed the beauty and naturalness of the sensual realm.

Ed EMSHWILLER

8 MIN. COLOR LIFELINES

Nude model and animated, abstract line drawings combine and clash in dynamic counterpoint, with both aesthetic and symbolic interest. Music by Teiji Ito. *The Creative Film Foundation Award of Distinction.*

5 MIN. THANATOPSIS

Image and sound are powerfully organized to express the feeling of internal anguish in this major experimental work. *Special Award, Experimental Film Festival, Belgium.*

Stan Vanderbeek

9 MIN. COLOR SCIENCE FRICTION

This non-verbal political satire, using pantomime and collage, reflects on mass society, conformism, and today's infatuation with rockets. *Award of Distinction, Creative Film Foundation. Highest Award, West German International Film Festival and Bergamo International Film Festival.*

4 MIN. COLOR SPHERICAL SPACE

A dance film made with Elaine Summers in which the nude figure is placed against nature—in this case, a particular and spherical sense of nature as produced by a special lens which takes in an 195° field of view on film.

TRIANGULAR

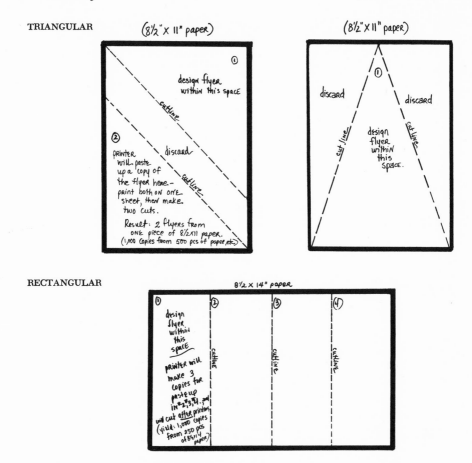

RECTANGULAR

Then again, designing your promotional in an odd shape to fit on a regular piece of paper or at an odd angle on the paper is attention-getting.

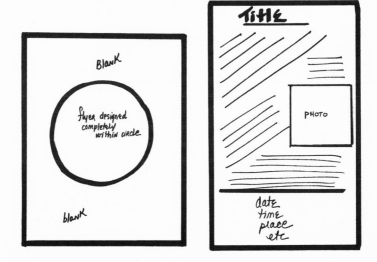

Be inventive. The flyers are bound to look amateurish at the outset, but that's O.K. You are amateurs. If your group prospers and survives, you soon won't be; and the longer you're in existence, the better your advertising will be.

Photo-offset is limited, but for the relatively small amount of money it costs, a lot can be done with it.

EXAMPLES OF PHOTOGRAPHS AND ADS

The following photos and ads will give you some idea of what types of promotional materials are available for your films from all different sources: catalogues, newspapers, the distributors themselves or from film periodicals.

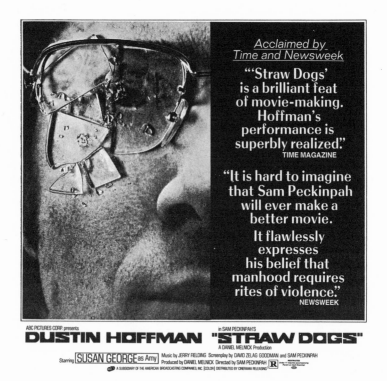

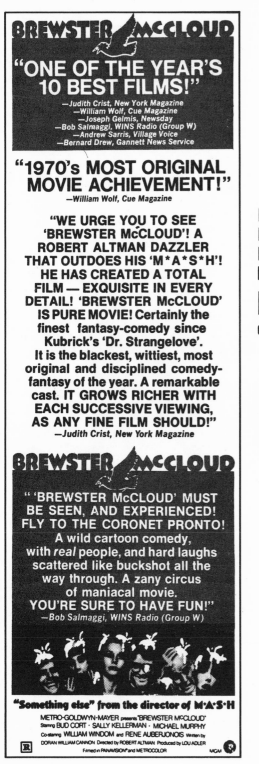

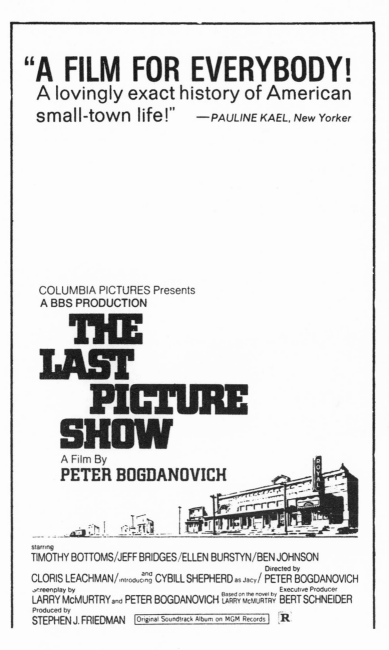

Drawing by David Levine. Reprinted with permission from The New York Review of Books. *Copyright © 1968 NYRev Inc.*

Doyle is
bad news—
but a
good
cop.

The time is just right for an out and out thriller like this.

THE
FRENCH CONNECTION

20TH CENTURY-FOX PRESENTS "THE FRENCH CONNECTION" A PHILIP D'ANTONI PRODUCTION
STARRING GENE HACKMAN FERNANDO REY ROY SCHEIDER TONY LO BIANCO MARCEL BOZZUFFI
DIRECTED BY WILLIAM FRIEDKIN PRODUCED BY PHILIP D'ANTONI ASSOCIATE PRODUCER KENNETH UTT
EXECUTIVE PRODUCER G. DAVID SCHINE SCREENPLAY BY ERNEST TIDYMAN MUSIC COMPOSED AND CONDUCTED BY DON ELLIS
COLOR BY DE LUXE

R RESTRICTED

The following promotionals are from distributors who supply the advertising campaign:

(These color mini-handouts and large color posters available in quantity.)

FILMS BY
JOHN
LENNON
YOKO
ONO

DUCK!

JULES FEIFFER'S
little
MURDERS
ELLIOT GOULD · DONALD SUTHERLAND · ALAN ARKIN

"Next time some xxxxxxxxxxR asks you for the time, bugaloo...away. Time ain't REAL nohow."

THE ORIGINAL LAST POETS

RIGHT ON!

If you're READy for it— right ON. If not— this movie could mess up your mind.

International Critics Prize
MANNHEIM FESTIVAL

Choice of Directors
CANNES FESTIVAL

PRINTING A SEASON ANNOUNCEMENT

Whenever you feel that your group is sufficiently organized and you've got some surplus funds, you might like to print up an announcement covering your program for an entire season's run, or half the run.

You can handle this in any number of ways, according to the promotional materials you have available for each film, the amount of money you can spend and the amount of time involved in the layout work.

The following formats are easily adapted to most any type of program:

A large poster (11 x 17), listing all the films for the season, with a miniature picture and a few words, either reviews or capsule story plots and the date for each title laid out like so:

Breaking the season into groups of films is also a good way to promote your shows, especially when running festivals.

THE CLASSIC
BOGART

Thurs. June 17 — Sun. June 20
CASABLANCA and BIG SLEEP

Mon. June 21 — Wed. June 23
PASSAGE TO and MARKED
MARSEILLES WOMAN

Thurs. June 24 — Sun. June 27
TREASURE OF and PETRIFIED
SIERRA MADRE FOREST

Mon. June 28 — Tues. June 29
HIGH and KING OF THE
SIERRA UNDERWORLD

THE CLASSIC
ZANIES

HARPO · GROUCHO · CHICO
MARX BROTHERS

TODAY THRU SAT.
A NIGHT AT THE OPERA
AND
AT THE CIRCUS

SUN. THRU WED.
A DAY AT THE RACES
AND
THE BIG STORE

THE CLASSIC
W.C. FIELDS

WED. & THURS.
TILLIE AND GUS
AND
MY LITTLE CHICKADEE

FRI. THRU SUN.
THE BANK DICK
AND
NEVER GIVE A SUCKER
AN EVEN BREAK

MON. & TUES.
THE OLD FASHIONED WAY
AND
YOU CAN'T CHEAT AN
HONEST MAN

TUES. & WED. JULY 14 & 15 — JEWELED HORROR TALE **The MAGICIAN** **&** INGMAR BERGMAN'S *Smiles of a* **SUMMER NIGHT** — CANNES FILM FESTIVAL WINNER

THURS.-MON. JULY 16-20 — ORSON WELLES' **CITIZEN KANE** **&** ALFRED HITCHCOCK'S **THE LADY VANISHES** — NEGLECTED MASTERPIECE

TUES. & WED. JULY 21 & 22 — JOSEF VON STERNBERG'S **The Blue Angel** **&** FRITZ LANG'S **M**

THURS.-MON. JULY 23-27 — JEAN RENOIR'S MASTERPIECE **GRAND ILLUSION** **&** RENE CLEMENT'S ANTI-WAR MASTERPIECE **FORBIDDEN GAMES**

TUES. & WED. JULY 28 & 29 — AKIRA KUROSAWA'S **RASHOMON** **&** SATYAJIT RAY'S **Two Daughters**

THURS.-MON. JULY 30-AUG. 3 — MARCEL CAMUS' **Black Orpheus** **&** SERGEI PARADJHANOV'S **SHADOWS of FORGOTTEN ANCESTORS**

TUES. & WED. AUG. 4 & 5 — SERGEI EISENSTEIN'S **POTEMKIN** **&** **ALEXANDER NEVSKY**

THURS.-MON. AUG. 6-10 — **SHOOT THE PIANO PLAYER** **&** FRANCOIS TRUFFANT'S *The 400 Blows*

TUES. & WED. AUG. 11 & 12 — ACADEMY AWARD WINNER **The VIRGIN SPRING** **&** INGMAR BERGMAN'S **The SILENCE**

THURS.-MON. AUG. 13-17 — IN COLOR KINUGASA'S **GATE of HELL** **&** **UGETSU**

TUES. & WED. AUG. 18 & 19 — **TOP HAT** **&** FRED ASTAIRE & GINGER ROGERS AT THEIR BEST IN **SWINGTIME**

THURS.-MON. AUG. 20-24 — MAX OPHULS' LEGENDARY **La Ronde** **&** JEAN RENOIR'S **Rules of the Game**

TUES. & WED. AUG. 25 & 26 — CLIVE DONNER'S **THE CARETAKER** **&** CAROL REED'S **ODD MAN OUT**

THURS.-MON. AUG. 27-31 — **Wild Strawberries** **&** INGMAR BERGMAN'S **The Seventh Seal**

TUES. & WED. SEPT. 1 & 2 — PART I **IVAN the TERRIBLE** **&** SERGEI EISENSTEIN'S WITH SCENES IN COLOR **IVAN the TERRIBLE** PART II

THURS.-MON. SEPT. 3-7 — ORSON WELLES' **The Magnificent Ambersons** **&** MICHELANGELO ANTONIONI'S **L'AVVENTURA**

TUES. & WED. SEPT. 8 & 9 — CLASSIC FANTASY **Beauty and the Beast** **&** JEAN COCTEAU'S **ORPHEUS**

THURS.-MON. SEPT. 10-14 — MERIAN C. COOPER'S **KING KONG** **&** **Room Service** THE **MARX BROTHERS**

TUES. & WED. SEPT. 15 & 16 — THROUGH A GLASS ACADEMY AWARD WINNER **DARKLY** INGMAR BERGMAN'S **&** **WINTER LIGHT**

THURS.-MON. SEPT. 17-21 — FRANCOIS TRUFFANT'S **JULES and JIM** **&** MARCEL CARNE'S **LE JOUR SE LEVE**

Simply listing dates, titles, directors and awards is another very effective way to list your program. This festival (see opposite page), composed mainly of Janus Films, was run in the summer at the Elgin Cinema in New York.

A *miniature program booklet* can be printed, sized about 4 x 5, with a separate page or more for each title. This type of advertising gives a much wider latitude in describing each film. You can include a lot of data that wouldn't fit on the large sheet announcements. There is room to tell something about the director or one of the principal actors, where the idea for the film came from, or any other interesting information you have.

For instance:

FILM SOCIETY PROGRAM
FALL SEMESTER

SEPTEMBER 1972						
SUN	MON	TUES	WED	THUR	FRI	SAT
					1	2
3	4	5	6	7	8	9
10	11	12	13	14	15	16
17	18	19	20	21	22	23
24	25	26	27	28	29	30

NOVEMBER 1972						
SUN	MON	TUES	WED	THUR	FRI	SAT
			1	2	3	4
5	6	7	8	9	10	11
12	13	14	15	16	17	18
19	20	21	22	23	24	25
26	27	28	29	30		

OCTOBER 1972						
SUN	MON	TUES	WED	THUR	FRI	SAT
1	2	3	4	5	6	7
8	9	10	11	12	13	14
15	16	17	18	19	20	21
22	23	24	25	26	27	28
29	30	31				

DECEMBER 1972						
SUN	MON	TUES	WED	THUR	FRI	SAT
					1	2
3	4	5	6	7	8	9
10	11	12	13	14	15	16
17	18	19	20	21	22	23
24/31	25	26	27	28	29	30

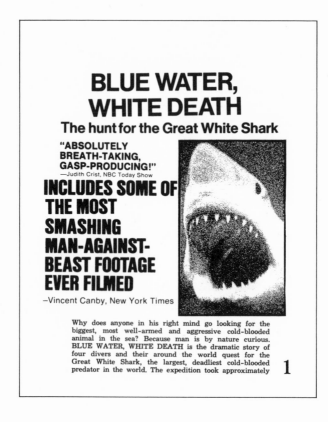

six months and covered more than 12,000 miles, including underwater locations in Ceylon, South Africa and Australia. "Spectacular, fascinating! BLUE WATER, WHITE DEATH is well worth seeing" —Stuart Klein, METROMEDIA. "Absolutely breath-taking, gasp producing!" —Judith Crist, NBC TODAY SHOW. "Truly Remarkable" —N.Y. TIMES. "Captivating!" —TIME MAGAZINE.

—United States—

"BOY"

A film by Nagisa Oshima

JAPAN

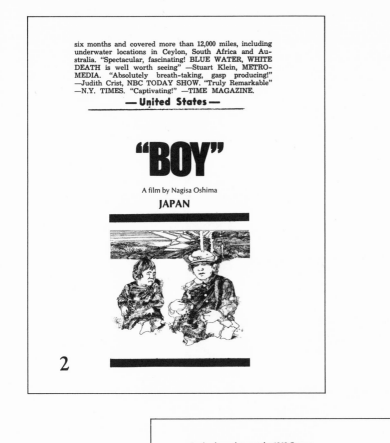

2

Boy has been shown at the 1969 Cannes Film Festival, 1969 New York Film Festival, 1969 San Francisco International Film Festival, 1969 Venice Film Festival, and 1969 London Film Festival.

"Extraordinary. Weird, beautiful, and terrifying. Undoubtedly the work of a major director." —The Observer (London)

"A very beautiful film…with great psychological truthfulness and rare penetration." —Le Monde

A haunting and, ultimately, terrifying film, Boy was "the foremost discovery" of last year's New York Film Festival, according to Newsweek which described it as the "study of an outlaw family in modern Japan that recalls Truffaut of The 400 Blows but really goes much further in penetrating individual psychology and portraying a society." Director Nagisa Oshima's story of a con game in which a boy is forced by his parents to throw himself in the path of automobiles can be seen as a mysterious thriller in disguise as well as a deeply poignant exploration of a child's fantasy world in conflict with reality.

With Fumio Watanabe, Tetsuo Abe, Akiko Koyama, Tsuyoshi Kinoshita

97 minutes, Eastmancolor, Cinemascope. Japanese with English subtitles. 3

"IT'S ALL IN THE MIND Y'KNOW!"
—GEORGE HARRISON

ELEVEN BEATLE SONGS

APPLE FILMS presents a KING FEATURES production

The Beatles "Yellow Submarine"

4

Starring SGT. PEPPER'S LONELY HEARTS CLUB BAND

Probably the outstanding popular hit of the recent Expo 67 in Montreal was the unusual triple-screen cartoon "Canada Is My Piano," the work of George Dunning, holder of six awards from outstanding world film festivals and perhaps the greatest behind-the-scenes master mind of motion picture animations in the business.

But, say those who know about such things, all his previous triumphs were merely warm-ups for his latest directorial stint, the Apple Films presentation and King Features production "Yellow Submarine," which "stars" animations of The Beatles

Based on a song by Beatles John Lennon and Paul McCartney, and offering four new Beatle hits as well as encores of at least 11 of their previous smashes, "Yellow Submarine" is said to be the first full-length animation ever made which employs animations of actual living performers. Among the non-living performers of the new epic is Sergeant Pepper's Lonely Hearts Club Band, also not among the unknowns of show biz.

Dunning, who perfected his craft with Norman McLaren, pioneer in the field of film animation and who had a hand in popularizing "Boing, Boing" a decade ago, is the founder of Canada's TV Cartoons, Ltd., which among other things has produced hundreds of TV commercials

for some of the world's largest sponsors, and a number of which have won prizes from Cannes to New York.

Many who have never heard the name Dunning have laughed hilariously at his comic titles in the Peter Sellers triumph "A Shot in the Dark" and more recently at those in "Inspector Clouseau." He has also produced the animated television series "Cool McCool" and "The Beatles" for King Features.

The new full-length animation is from a screenplay by Lee Minoff with assistance from Brodax, Jack Mendelsohn and Erich Segal, the latter a Yale professor of Roman and Greek classics who has been making a name for himself as a writer of high comedy lately.

The three new Beatle melodic hits which Dunning has skillfully woven into the fast-moving comedy animation are "All Too Much," "Altogether Now" and "Northern Song."

RUNNING TIME: 85 MINUTES

—Great Britain—

5

DUSTIN HOFFMAN

'**LITTLE BIG MAN**'

CO-STARRING

CHIEF DAN GEORGE

6

Sole survivor of Custer's last stand at Little Big Horn, adopted Indian brave complete with braids and war paint, trapper, mule skinner, town drunk, and gunfighter (The Sodey Pop Kid) . . . these are just a few of the amazing characterizations of Jack Crabb portrayed so brilliantly by Dustin Hoffman in LITTLE BIG MAN. "The '70's first great epic!" —TIME MAGAZINE
Dustin Hoffman, who holds two Academy Award nominations for THE GRADUATE, and MIDNIGHT COWBOY, totally captivates his audience in what the critics have acclaimed as "A genuine mark of genius!" —John Schubeck, ABC-TV. "A rich, illuminating, moving piece of art." —Charles Champlin, L.A. Times. "Stingent and powerful!" —Judith Crist "A big funny, exciting movie." —Leonard Harris, CBS-TV. The praise is endless!

139 minutes   directed by Arthur Penn

— United States —

7

The last two pages could be devoted to a concise schedule for easy reference, the place of the showing and any information you would wish to include about your group

Inside rear cover

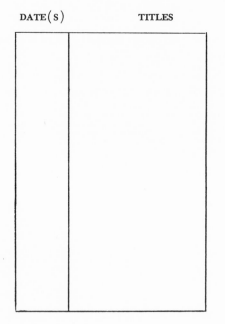

DATE(S)   TITLES

The full season announcement sheets and the booklet are excellent devices with which to launch a membership drive. Even if large numbers don't respond by buying a season ticket, you are presenting your entire program to as many people as possible at school and in the community who will have the schedule at home or in their office for future reference. People tend to forget that they have an alternative in movie entertainment other than what is offered at commercial theaters. If they're presented with a definite advance listing, they will no doubt come back at least a few times during the season.

PROMOTION

The following guidelines will be of some help to high-school, college and university groups that wish to attract an audience not only from their own schools but also from other campuses in the area and from the general community as well. Of course local circumstances will largely dictate the emphasis the promotional campaign assumes.

The promotional campaign for the first film of a series, or a single film screening, should be begun a full two weeks in advance of the show date. Basically the idea is to have posters and/or handbills in every location where potential customers will notice them.

ON CAMPUS

Posters or flyers should be on every bulletin board, concentrating on first floors of buildings and the *main* areas of congregation.

Stacks of flyers should be placed in cafeterias, lounges, libraries, dorms, etc.

Teachers who are sympathetic to the cause should definitely be given announcements. Quite possibly they will announce the film to their classes. (This is especially important when the film is a course-related title.)

Notices should be placed in the campus newspaper, whose entertainment editor may wish to write his weekly column on your film, and in the faculty news bulletin.

If an event occurs on the campus that attracts a large number of people (even another film society's screening), go there and hand out miniature announcements.

OFF CAMPUS

This can be done only when the contractual agreement with the distributor of a film allows for outside advertising.

Notices should be placed at high schools and other college campuses in the area, on bulletin boards, in campus news letters, bulletins, etc. Place flyers in high-density areas such as cafeterias and lounges around town.

Notices can be placed in store windows, health-food shops, supermarkets, clothing stores, restaurants, bookstores, bicycle shops, art-supply stores, art galleries, museums and libraries.

Any mailing lists that can be obtained from cultural-activities groups in town should be utilized.

Definitely place a notice in the public-events column that all newspapers have for non-profit organizations. The entertainment editor may wish to help by running a story with or without a clip from the film, announcing the screening. Perhaps a preview can be arranged so he may review the film in his column. Perhaps your group can afford the cost of a small ad on the movie page. Most radio stations allow time to non-profit organizations for public-service announcements. Distribute announcements to all stations.

There is no such thing as overpromoting. The more people you reach, the better your turnout will be—provided, of course, you reach the right people in the right places. Meaning only this: If you're advertising a general-entertainment film, you work equally at promoting in all the afore-mentioned places. But if you're running a film that has appeal to a specialized audience—for instance a rock movie—you'll want to promote especially hard at high schools and record stores, and use public-service announcement or paid radio advertising. An anthropological film that also has great appeal to the general moviegoer should be promoted heavily to anthropology teachers at colleges and high schools, museums and libraries. A sophisticated foreign-language film would mean bringing the title to the attention of teachers in the foreign-language departments at colleges and high schools. Also museums and library distribution deserves extra attention. These special pushes are in addition to the procedures mentioned before.

Of course if there is a film department of *any* sort—movie-making, movie appreciation, etc.—the people involved should be kept right up to date on what you are doing. The most essential place to promote is at your film screenings. Everyone who attends should at least be presented with an announcement of next week's movie. Preferably they should all be given a season program. Just leaving stacks of these around is not enough. The ticket-taker should distribute them to every person.

Groups that are interested in drawing an audience only from a distinct community—i.e., a college group wishing a response from their students and faculty—have a much easier time of it. The off-campus running around becomes unnecessary.

Groups that are completely subsidized (not dependent on admissions for support) are indeed in fortunate circumstances. All the pressure is off. The movie is for free. The announcements are out. The longevity of the organization will not be determined only by the size of the crowd.

Film societies are and will always be criticized for their advertising techniques. Some people seem to feel it's not "sensitive" to promote a movie aggressively. What they fail to recognize is that if no one comes, no group. And if no group, no more movies.

It would be lovely to hand-letter ten announcements on delicate pastel paper and paste these notices shyly out of sight on bulletin boards so as not to offend anyone's delicacy. It would be fine, except that most groups can't survive financially with a timid approach. The club is not a business, but it must be run much like one if it is to achieve any tenure. This demands confident, aggressive advertising. Fortunately, the value of film societies is recognized by most people, and they will get behind your group in every way they can; but there are others—the non-doers, the criticizers—who feel that it is their moral duty to rip down your announcements; that they are sensitive and real film appreciators and would not promote so outlandishly. They are, of course, jealous. Petty jealousies are hard to deal with and they crop up quite a lot on campuses, deserved or not. The most frequent accusation is that you are making a fortune, or else you wouldn't be working so hard at promoting. Fifty percent of all gross receipts go to the distributor (sometimes sixty to sixty-five percent). Another twenty-five percent goes directly for shipping, advertising, hall rental, projector rental and paid help. Whatever is left, if indeed there is any money left, is not pocketed by a few greedy individuals licking their chops but goes for stationery, equipment improvements, an office, a mailing list, more publications and film books. Running a film society is not a low-keyed affair. Unless you are in the blessed position of having your expenses for the season paid for in advance by subscription membership or the group is completely subsidized, there is always the pressure of advertising to think about. Have we promoted enough? What if no one comes? What will we do next week? There are instances when the officers of a film society will hire a manager at a base salary plus a percentage of the gross receipts for each show. He is in charge of the promoting as well as the physical running of the show, and being paid in this fashion gives him the added incentive to advertise thoroughly indeed —a very workable arrangement. Enthusiasm for stapling posters on bulletin boards can certainly wane if not altogether vanish when repeated again and again. A person who is being paid according to how many people show up is a distinct advantage to the group that is solely dependent on weekly admissions for survival.

Soliciting subscription memberships is very difficult unless you are the only film society around. If you are not, which is usually the case now on college campuses, you'll have to be decidedly aggressive. Remember that people will not put their money behind an unknown program no matter how entertainment-starved they are.

In order to insure any success you must print a season announcement. Any kind will do, as professional as you can make it within your budgetary means. The back page of a booklet or bottom part of announcement should be devoted to information regarding subscription members:

The _____ Film Society has been formed for the purpose of screening films not regularly available at the commercial theaters in this neighborhood.

The fifteen films listed in this booklet have been chosen because we believe (according to the critical acclaim we have researched for each title) they represent the best examples of creativity in both contemporary and classic cinema.

We are a non-profit organization, solely dependent on your financial support for our continuity. As an advantage to you and to ourselves, we prefer that you purchase a season membership ticket.

Single admission for each film is $1.25. Over fifteen shows, this would total $18.75. The season ticket costs $15, so should you choose to subscribe, as we hope you will, there is a saving of $3.75, or the price of three movies.

Our advantage is obviously financial security. If we can obtain the support of enough individuals who will buy subscription memberships, our budget will be met, and we can relax from the worries and pressures of promotion; have more time to research films, prepare program notes, improve our technical presentation; and concentrate on the film show as an arena of art instead of as a quasi-business.

This group can continue to exist only with your financial support.

In addition to the movie discount, as a subscribing member you will have free access to the club's cinema periodicals and books, stored at _____.

Any help you can offer is certainly appreciated and if you would especially like to see a certain film, please do tell us about it.

The following form can be filled out and presented with a check for $15 to the girl at the front ticket desk, or mailed to:

_____

_____

_____

Your membership card will be mailed before our next show.
THANK YOU!

Now you're offering something tangible. But people still have to be talked into subscribing. You cannot just hand them a promotional brochure and expect them all to whip out the cash immediately. At your first screening, when you launch the subscription membership drive, you should have several (five on up, according to the crowd) congenial persons (aside from the ticket seller and taker who initially distribute the brochures) who go over and talk to each and every person who attends. It's nice to have a coffee hour after the film to do the selling, but so many people slip out immediately after a movie is over, you're better off to approach them before the film. Try to persuade them to subscribe for the season. Do they like the program? If "yes," then they'll save $_____ by subscribing, plus the benefit to themselves. Further point out that they will be actively helping to sustain a valuable cultural program for the community. If they say they don't like the program, that's no cause for alarm. I have heard people's opinions of films change in sixty seconds. Point out the reviews, the actors, the awards, the overall slant of the program, the cinematic techniques employed which deserve their attention. Present the program as a well-thought-out movie experience you have intended it to be, explaining all the while that the schedule represents the best consensus of local opinion and critics' national reviews that are available.

If it's "no," it's "no." You can't persuade people who don't want to subscribe because they 1) don't have that much money to lay out in advance, 2) will not come to more than half the films anyhow so know they aren't saving any money, or 3) just hate to get "involved" with anything.

But personally approaching each person about subscribing is essential if you want to produce any results from your campaign. If your goal is 500 members and you manage to subscribe 250 you're doing very well. You still continue charging at-the-door admissions, so nothing is lost.

Brochures advertising membership should be liberally sprinkled around at places where people whose arms don't need to be twisted will voluntarily subscribe through the mails—museums, art galleries, bookstores and the like. You will want to advertise your films at these places anyhow, so the effort is sure to produce at least extra attendance if not the desired result of subscribing members. People who join clubs value their membership cards. It should be designed as nicely as possible, with numbers on the bottom representing the shows so the cards can be punched for each week they are used. What you do about unscrupulous card users is your affair. If they become too frequent and it's too difficult to keep things under control, better forget subscription memberships for the next season. For instance, if you've sold 250 subscriptions and 100 people lost their cards, it's a fair guess that maybe five really did lose them, and the other ninety-five are looking to get a free card to give away or sell.

If the overall response is not good but you are managing to draw an adequate crowd each week, I would shelve the idea of maintaining subscriptions.

Modified approaches can be utilized, such as selling any six films in a season for a discount; or selling a series ticket, three in a row for the price of two, etc.

MEMBERSHIPS

Membership cards can be sold anywhere from $.25 to $1 apiece, or they can be given away. One reason for selling them is that you can use the funds to support a mailing list. You can mail once a week, bimonthly or monthly, depending on how much money you have allocated for this. Mailing lists that have been compiled from your own patrons are very good devices for promoting. When people receive an announcement of an event at their home or office addressed to them they tend to read it more thoroughly and will perhaps tack it up where other people you have no way of reaching can see it. End results—more returnees and more interest in your club. Many film societies give away or sell for a mere $.25 a membership card to each person that attends one of their film screenings as a means of evading the strict rules some distributors have about who may attend.

AT-THE-DOOR ADMISSIONS

The easiest way to go about collecting money is to charge admissions at each show. Some distributors stipulate that only members of that film club or persons at the school where the film is being shown can attend the screening. Others encourage the promotion of their titles to the outside community. Check your distributor's ruling concerning advertising very carefully.

Certainly local circumstances will largely dictate your methods of promotion. The idea is to advertise as extensively as possible within the legal boundaries of the contracts made with distributors. I have never heard of a group being fined $5,000 for violating this rule, but groups have been cut off from renting films and consequently put out of operation when they consistently abused this clause in their contracts with distributors who specifically prohibit off-campus advertising.

Some groups, finding themselves so restricted by the rulings for non-theatrical screening, break away from their original base of operations and form small art theaters where the patronage is large enough to support such ventures.

Thorough advertising is absolutely essential to the success of a film society. The more people that know about the screening, the better the attendance will be. Keep in mind the restrictions, and do the most thorough job possible.

6

Running the Show

Friendly presentation and technical perfection are the keynotes to aim for. Imparting an atmosphere of validity and efficiency to each and every film screening will enable the audience as a group to relax.

Generally speaking, even very independent-type people enjoy assuming a passive attitude in a darkened movie theater. Once the lights go out they can laugh or cry or jeer or sob or moan or not react at all. They become anonymous (a relief for even the most independent) within the sheltered confines of the cave.

The time from when they buy their ticket to when the film actually goes on the screen is, however, an agitated interval. The expectation level is high, and optimism is right there waiting to be expanded. Everybody is looking at everybody else, and those among us who turn on to crowds find ourselves stimulated. What potential for attracting attention to ourselves! And indeed our behavior is socially ritualistic during this interlude. I often think it is not at all different from when we were in elementary school and all the kids from all the grades were in one large auditorium waiting for the principal to appear and the assembly to begin. What hysteria, insane giggling, running up and down the aisles, tickling, punching, or making our best friends laugh—absolute frenzy during that ten- to fifteen-minute period of time. Since most film-society screenings take place in school auditoriums of one sort or another, it's not surprising that

91

we react like ten- and eleven-year-olds. It happens at commercial movie theaters also, but the overwhelming feeling there is maintaining a social role, which is not particularly true of film societies. A lot of the frenzy derives from the fact that by coming to a movie people free themselves of any responsibility. They don't have to *do* anything. They've already paid; nothing more is expected of them. Often the people who run the screening have nothing to do with this mood. It arises of itself, generated by the interacting chemistry of the entire audience. Other times a crowd needs to be pampered, coaxed and reassured in ways other than words that all is well and they can relax. Then again, for no apparent reason, a crowd can be sullen, withdrawn and nonreactive. Ringling Brothers' three-ring circus couldn't crack their mood. They won't talk, laugh, clap, cough or even move in their chairs. The mood is infectious. One never knows if they're enjoying themselves or not.

Remember that it is difficult for most people to relax. They almost have to be tricked into letting go of that external world with all its problems and responsibilities. The reason they're coming to a movie at all is because they want to forget it all. By helping them shed their reality for two hours you'll help yourselves, because they'll come back hoping it will happen again.

THE FACILITY

It doesn't much matter where you hold your screenings. Even the most dreadful-looking auditorium can be made remarkably cheerful with the addition of potted plants, incense, movie posters and background music. You simply obtain the best facility that you can use regularly, and go from there to correct the imperfections as well as you can. The film, after all, is the thing.

The first factor to be considered when choosing an auditorium is the rental fee for non-profit groups. This should be under $50. For profit-making groups, generally $50 to $100. The next consideration is the projection facilities. Built-in projectors are best. If there is none, is there a projection booth where portable machines have a platform to stand on? If not, is there enough room at the rear to mount portable machines on high tables? (A word of caution: Make sure electric outlets are in the rear.)

Test the sound system with a reliable film. Crackling, breaking or fuzziness indicates trouble. However, you can bring in your own speaker and extension cord each week, so this is not crucial, although it is decidedly more convenient to obtain a good sound system.

Older auditoriums in particular tend to absorb sound. Seat yourself in different places—front, rear, left rear, etc. Can you hear clearly wherever you sit? This *is* crucial.

Since, with some distributors, the fee for a film jumps considerably for multiple exhibitions, obtaining a large facility (400 to 500 seats) and holding fewer screenings is more desirable than a 200-seat theater where you must hold many screenings. Wooden seats get awfully hard after the first hour; soft seats are a pleasure.

The screen is important. Beaded glass screens reflect well to people who are in a direct visual line. People sitting off either to the right or left have half their visibility cut. A lenticular screen (flat white) reflects equally well to left, center and right spectators.

Be sure there is a good air-conditioning/heating system. A stuffy auditorium is no fun. Being cold isn't half so bad, but you don't want people to have to wear overcoats either.

Be *assured* that the use of the auditorium is on a *regular* basis.

Look for a hall that has an alternative to full-on, harsh, bright classroom lighting. If you can't locate one, perhaps there is a chance of installing a rheostat (dimmer knob) in the hall.

Inspect the toilet facilities and see if there is adequate parking space nearby. It is also important to have a refreshment stand or vending machines close by.

If you can locate an auditorium that satisfactorily fits all the above specifications, you are indeed fortunate. If not, there are ways to remedy even the most appalling circumstances, except *acoustics*. If the acoustics are bad, don't use that hall. It will drive the audience crazy to keep straining to understand the sound track.

Hard surfaced walls and ceiling, such as plaster, reflect sound waves and make sound harsh. Set sound volume at a moderate level and tone toward treble.

Acoustical treatment of a ceiling absorbs sufficient sound to provide comfortable, distinct, hearing. Drapes and upholstered furniture likewise absorb sound and make listening more pleasing.

(Courtesy Kalart/Victor)

If the *sound* is bad, rent or borrow a twelve- to fifteen-inch speaker. Have an extension cord made by buying as many feet of regular house lamp wiring as you need to reach from the speaker to the projector, placing the speaker on a table at the front of the auditorium. Affix a standard one-fourth-inch male phone plug to the end that fits the speaker and a five-eighths-inch male jack to the end that plugs into the rear of the projector. (This size for Bell and Howell; Kodak machine.)

If there is no screen or the screen is unsuitable, probably one can be rented nearby, or perhaps a school can lend you one.

If you are running a CinemaScope (wide-screen) film, there is no chance that the image will fit on a regular rectangular movie screen. You can either rent two screens, placing one on either side of the center screen, or, if there's enough support, top and bottom. Or you can buy two double-bed-size white sheets and tack them up, one on either side.

If there are no built-in projection facilities, provided you have the proper height clearance, tables can be built to support portable machines.

As for seating capacity, 200 seats should be the minimum. Multiple screenings can be held. However, seriously figure out how much it will cost for each extra screening as opposed to how many people will attend each performance. The larger the hall, the better; fewer screenings, lower minimum guarantee.

If the hall is attractive, the lack of intermediate lighting is not too crucial; but if it is an eyesore, avoid depressing the audience. If you cannot have a dimmer switch installed, a way around blasting people with harsh light is to hold a continuous slide show while people are being seated. This will throw enough light so that people can find their way around.

A fair guide to the rental fee is not to spend more than $.15 per customer.

If your first choice for a hall cannot be booked in advance for regularly scheduled screenings, try your second choice. If you have the same problem there, then your alternative is to take what you can get when you can get it.

A stuffy auditorium in the summer months is intolerable. Open the doors for free flow of air. As for being too cold—well, people *can* wear their coats. It's not as bad as a steaming crowd.

Groups that operate on college or high-school campuses won't have too much difficulty finding an adequate facility. For groups that aren't campus-based there are a number of places to look into—community centers, churches, YMCAs, museums, libraries, out of doors, barns, warehouses. Also *always* check out the possibility of using the local schools' auditoriums. The main thing is doing the best with what you have. People who attend film-society screenings are more interested in the *film* than they are in a super-slick presentation. If you're uneasy about the facility, you can put out a mimeoed fact sheet to be distributed to the audience explaining the limitations and the improvements you hope to make when you have sufficient funds.

The people needed to run the show are a ticket-seller, a ticket-taker (also distributor of program notes and announcements), projectionist and manager (also announcer).

According to the size of the group, there can be four different individuals who handle each of the above tasks, or you can consolidate the duties among fewer people, such as ticket-seller and taker, projectionist–manager, or ticket-seller–manager, ticket-taker–projectionist.

Whoever sells the tickets is one of the persons everybody remembers. Consequently he or she should be congenial, efficient and not easily irritated. The whole attitude of the film society is represented in the actions of this person. Part of the appeal of film societies is that they are more personal. This should be reflected in the attitude of the cashier. The cashier's main functions are making proper change and keeping a careful record of the number of tickets sold. Numbered tickets should be used so that at any given point you know how many seats have been sold and how much money should be in the till after the last person has entered. You will need exact figures for tax purposes and for figuring out the distributor's percentage.

The ticket-taker has to make sure no one is sneaking in for free and also distribute the season program and the advertisement for next week's show. He should hold the first and last ticket stub as a check on the cashier.

The projectionist's job is to arrive at least forty-five minutes before the beginning of the screening, set up the film, check the sound, make sure the show will start on time and monitor radio, tapes, phono or slides in the interim.

The manager should oversee all these activities, helping out wherever needed. For instance, if a group of people are holding up the ticket line by querying the cashier in detail about the film, he should take them aside and answer all the questions they have so the starting time of the show won't be delayed. He should likewise help people find seats when the hall becomes crowded. He should be a competent projectionist in the event the projectionist doesn't show, becomes ill or needs help to solve a problem. He should keep spare parts easily accessible: replacement bulbs, splicing kit, etc. After about 90 percent of the crowd has been admitted, the manager should make a brief introductory speech about the film to be screened that night and talk a little about the films to be presented in the future. He should also mention other films being offered by film societies and theaters in the neighborhood. Other events of interest should be announced—a benefit rock concert, the opening of a bookstore, etc. He or she should be a good public speaker to carry this off well. By the time these announcements have been completed, everyone will be admitted and the show can begin.

For a relatively small sum of money you can provide, at no charge to your customers, popcorn during the movie and coffee afterward. You might ask your local health-food shop if they are interested in selling sandwiches, pastries, dried fruit, nuts and juices at your showings.

Providing a small selection of film periodicals for sale to your patrons will be appreciated. All these extra details are the responsibility of the entire organization.

A competent projectionist makes all the difference. It's a seemingly dull, simple job, but it does require constant attention. A projectionist's best friend is a pair of cheap binoculars. Have your films checked and cleaned before the night of screening for broken sprocket holes, bad splices and excessive dirt that may clog your projector gate. The film should be in focus on the screen, to be in clear focus to the entire audience. When 16mm prints are made from 35mm materials very often the focusing of these prints must be adjusted ten or more times during one film. Likewise, the quality of the sound varies. Tone and volume must be continually readjusted to insure maximum clarity. Before you hire a projectionist, test him out first so you know he *knows* what he's doing.

The audience cares about three things: the clarity of the sound, the focus of the film and whether reel changes are smooth.

The following checklists and precautions supplied by the Kalart/Victor projector manufacturers may be helpful in the event of technical difficulties:

POINTS TO CHECK

No Light
1. Motor and lamp switches (*both* must be on)
2. Operating lever (must be up)
3. Lamp (burned out if filament is broken)
4. Power cord and/or extension (conductor may be broken or have defective contacts)
5. Room outlet (may not have power—check fuse)

Poor Image
1. Focus
2. Room light (may be excessive on screen)
3. Screen (may be defective, inadequate or dirty)
4. Film surface (may be scratched)
5. Optical system (lenses may be dirty)
6. Line voltage (may be too low)
7. Extension cord (may be too light or too long)

SOUND PROBLEMS

No Sound
1. Amplifier (may not be on or warmed up)
2. Exciter lamp (may be burned out)
3. Film (may be silent—with two rows of sprocket holes)
4. Speaker cable (may be defective or not connected)
5. Press reset (may be tripped)
6. Sound drum (may not be properly seated)

Poor or Weak Sound
1. Controls (volume or tone may not be set properly)
2. Room (acoustics may be faulty)
3. Sound lens (may be dirty)
4. Film (may be defective)
5. Sound-silent switch (may be in silent position)
6. Speaker cable (may have loose conductor)
7. Line voltage (may be too low)
8. Speaker (may be placed too low or too close to wall)
9. Rear impedance roller (may be stuck)

CARE OF FILM

Whenever possible, avoid projection of dirty film. Dirt, oil and emulsion may be deposited on channels and roller and eventually cause scratching. Dirty film will also result in reduced screen brilliance and definition as well as loss in sound quality and volume.

Immediately following the running of such film, carefully clean all film channels, rollers, tips, etc. To clean film, place film on rewind and draw on rewind, drawing it slowly between a soft lintless cloth or pads well saturated with film cleaner. Frequently change cloth or pad surfaces and remoisten with film cleaner as they become charged with film soil.

For Kodachrome and Ansco color film, use same procedure as above, but only with a small quantity of film cleaner, since it is possible to soften the emulsion of Kodachrome and Ansco color film.

Occasionally new prints just out of the processing laboratory are "green"—a condition of stickiness that may cause "jumpy" pictures, loss of loop or noisy projection. The same condition may occur with films that have been over humidified. Such film may be conditioned by exposure of the reel to the air for at least twelve hours for partial drying. Another expedient is to run the film through the projector at sixteen-frame silent speed, with projector and exciter lamps on, and with the projection lens gate open.

Don't allow film to remain on projector after showing. Always immediately replace in film can.

Don't pull end of film to tighten on reel, since this may cause scratching. Never place film on radiators, thus causing drying and consequently warped, brittle film.

Always keep spare take-up reels clean and in dustproof containers. Also remove any dust on inside reel surface before using. Dust transferred to film and in film channels causes scratches.

For those who must rent projectors, screens, sound system and all connecting cords, the following advice should prove helpful (courtesy Kalart/Victor Corporation):

ROOM ARRANGEMENT

Today, 16mm sound programs are in such wide use that rooms in which projectors are used may not always be acoustically correct for showing sound films. This section is presented as a guide to help compensate for imperfect room conditions.

Projector placement. First row of seats should be no closer to screen than two and one-half times the screen width. The last row of seats should be no farther away than six times the screen width.

Locate projector at rear of audience, omitting center aisle. To provide for comfortable viewing, avoid area too near screen and beyond thirty degrees to either side.

A good rule for screen size is: Screen width equals one-sixth the distance from projector to screen. (See projection lens table.)

Speaker placement. Do not place speaker on floor. For ideal placement, the speaker should be diagonally in front of audience (preferably in a corner) at head height or slightly above. If space or time is at a premium, the projector may be operated with its own speaker.

With time and experience you will be able to perfect your presentation. Never walk into a show cold without going through a trial run. It takes

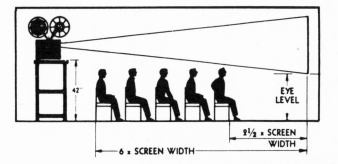

Focal Length of Lens	DISTANCE OF PROJECTOR FROM SCREEN IN FEET															
	1'	2'	3'	4'	5'	6'	8'	10'	15'	20'	30'	40'	50'	75'	100'	150'
	WIDTH OF PICTURE															
⅝"	7"	14"	22"	29"	36"	43"	59"	6'1"	9'1"	12'2"	18'3"	24'3"	30'4"	....	....	....
¾"	6"	12"	18"	24"	30"	37"	49"	5'1"	7'7"	10'2"	15'3"	20'4"	25'5"	....	....	....
1"	4"	9"	13"	18"	22"	27"	36"	45"	5'8"	7'7"	11'4"	15'2"	19'0"	....	....	....
1½"	4"	6"	9"	12"	15"	18"	24"	30"	45"	5'0"	7'7"	10'1"	12'8"	....	....	....
2"	2"	4"	6"	9"	11"	13"	18"	22"	34"	45"	5'8"	7'7"	9'6"	14'3"	19'0"	28'5"
2½"	....	3"	5"	7"	9"	11"	14"	18"	27"	36"	54"	6'1"	7'7"	12'8"	16'5"	22'9"
3"	....	3"	4"	6"	7"	9"	12"	15"	22"	30"	45"	5'0"	6'4"	9'6"	12'8"	19'0"
3½"	....	2"	4"	5"	6"	7"	10"	13"	19"	26"	39"	52"	5'5"	8'1"	10'10"	16'3"
4"	....	2"	3"	4"	5"	6"	9"	11"	17"	22"	34"	45"	57"	7'1"	9'6"	14'3"

Determine picture size, projection distance and proper lens according to this table.

time to set up even when you're familiar with the place. When working with a strange auditorium there may be many modifications necessary which can't be carried through at the last minute.

Many film societies that are well established choose to buy their equipment rather than rent. An added benefit is knowing that you will be using equipment that isn't faulty. Sixteen millimeter rental projectors get thrown around a lot; consequently there always seems to be something wrong with them. Of course when you have your own you're completely responsible for maintenance and purchasing bulbs. Most popular 16mm portable machines are quite reliable, hence maintenance is not too costly. Bulbs are expensive, but the added benefit is that you won't be showing a film with a bulb that has only an hour to go. This has very dim image and can blow out at any time during the reel. Very annoying. Many clubs that rent their projectors buy bulbs anyhow to be assured of maximum screen brilliance and dependability, as their schools or rental companies can't supply them with high-wattage bulbs or bulbs that have only a few hours left. Bell & Howell, Kalart, Kodak, and RCA are the largest manufacturers of portable 16mm projectors. Prices vary considerably. You get what you pay for. Some are intended for classroom use but can be used in an auditorium; others are designed for use specifically in auditoriums.

BELL & HOWELL

(Complete information regarding your nearest sales representative is available from Bell & Howell, A/V Products Division, 7100 McCormick Road, Chicago, Illinois, 60645.)

Model #1545

(Suggested retail price: $721 plus tax)
Small to medium-sized auditoriums

Automatic Threading
Automatic Reel-to-Reel Threading
    onto Autoload 400′ Reels
Synchronized Automatic Loop
    Restorer
Systems Restorer
Reverse Control
Drum Focusing
Compact, Trim Modern Design
Snap-On Lamp House Cover
Direct Drive Blower

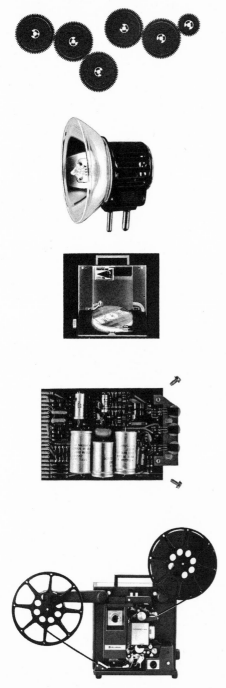

Silent and Sound Speeds
3 Interruption Shutter
All Gear Drive
Whisper-Quiet Operation
Factory Sealed Lubrication
Time-Proven Autoload Film
  Transport System
Precision Frame Control
Swing-Out Gate
Carbo-Nitride Treated Guide Rails
Stellite Shuttle
2″ F/1.6 Lens
Built-In Film Leader Trimmer
Low Center of Gravity for
  Maximum Stability
25-Hour/250 Watt Tungsten-Halogen
  Lamp with Integral
  Dichroic Reflector
350 Watt Total Power Consumption
  U.L. Approved
All Metal (Die-Cast Aluminum) Case
Integral Speaker
One-Hand Precision Tilt Knob
Jack for Auxiliary Speaker (8 ohms)
Enclosed Storage Compartment for
  Cord, Reel, Spare Lamps
Plug-In Solid State Amplifier with
  Integrated Circuit
No Warm-Up Time for Amplifier
Transformer Isolated Amplifier
10 Watt (RMS) Output
Accepts Reels from 400′ to 2,000′
Folding, Gear Driven Reel Arms with
  Push-Button Position Detent
Push-Button Actuated Fast Rewind
Functionally Located Controls

Accessories:
Accessory F/1.4 Lens—
  1-1/2″ to 4″ Inclusive
Accessory 5/8″ and 1″ Lenses
Accessory Zoom Lens Attachment
  Fits 1-1/2″ to 3″ Lenses
Accessory Anamorphic Lens
  Attachment Fits 1-1/2″ to 3″
  Lenses

Bell & Howell has machines whose prices vary from $691 to $1,620. Your local distributor might offer a discount.

In addition to their machines for films that have optical sound tracks, Bell & Howell manufactures a machine for projecting films with *magnetic and optical* sound tracks. This machine can also be used to record sound tracks on films that have a blank 16mm magnetic strip.

The Bell & Howell Magnetic-Recording 16MM High-Fidelity Sound Projector Model 8302L

(Suggested retail price: $1,195)

2″ S/1.6 Super Proval Lens
Built-In 4″ × 6″ Front-Mounted Oval Speaker
Powerful 10-Watt Amplifier
1000 Watt Lamp
Straight Line Optical System
Reverse and Still Picture Projection
Silent or Sound Speeds (18 or 24 F.P.S.)
Fool-Proof Threading
Pilot Light
Finger-Tip Controls
Fast Rewind
Top Mounted Reel Arms
105-129 Volt, 50-60 Hz, AC Only
Phono Jacks
Includes Dynamic Microphone, Spare Reel, and 50 Ft. Roll of Sound-striped Practice Film
Weight—38 lbs.
Dimensions—11″ W, 17-3/4″ L, 15-3/4″ H
U.L. Approved

KALART

(Complete information regarding your nearest sales office is available from Kalart/Victor Corporation, Plainville, Connecticut, 06062.)

Model #75–25

(Suggested retail price: $787)
Small to medium-sized auditoriums.

Amplifier

75-25, 25 Watt, RMS, Full Power Output

Separate tuning for treble and bass

Frequency response curve is flat from 100 to 18,000 cycles

Built-in Connections

Individual Microphone and Phonograph jacks with separate volume controls (75-25)

Single and Dual Speakers

Speakers

75-15 Built-in 5″ × 7″ door speaker with 50 ft. speaker cord

75-25 Separately cased 12″ speaker with 75 ft. speaker cord

75-15 Separately cased 12″ speaker with 75 ft. speaker cord

Projection Lamp

Up to 1200 watt

750 watt supplied as standard equipment

Light output—500 lumens on screen with Mark II shutter and 1000 watt lamp

Still Pictures

Automatic heat absorbing optical glass filter protects film and permits brilliant projection of selected frames

Improved optics for brighter, sharper picture

Operation

All controls conveniently located

Rapid power rewind—no belts or reels to change

Lens swings out 180° for easy cleaning and threading

Single drive sprocket—equal tension on film moving both in and out of projector

Top mounted reels—set projector on any surface without reel overhang

Once a year lubrication

Color coded threading path

Compensating film shoes automatically adjust for varying film thickness and splices

Large fan and heat-absorbing filters prevent over-heating

Heavy duty induction motor

Standard Equipment Supplied

Snap-out reel arms (2000' capacity) with built-in long life belts

750 watt projection lamp, ASA Code DDB

2"f:1.6 lens

1600' reel

Oiling kit

Film Movement Control

Sound Speed

Silent Speed

Forward

Reverse

Sound System

Heavy duty exciter lamp helps prevent distortion

Stationary sound drum—no moving parts to get out of adjustment

Sound lens depth of focus assures highest quality reproduction

Safety Film Trips

Protect against costly film damage

Film Pull Down

Self aligning—prevents torn sprocket holes

Sapphire tipped for lifetime wear

Kalart also manufactures a machine that will record magnetic sound tracks as well as play both optical and magnetic tracks. (Suggested retail price: $1,347. Model #70-25 MC3.) Their model has the MARC 300 high-intensity lighting system.

(*Note:* Kalart does not manufacture an automatic threading machine. However, they do guarantee that their machines will not damage film.)

For those of you who show or would like to show in 35mm, the above may be of interest.

Kodak and RCA manufacture comparable machines. RCA has a model that is designed so that three or four full reels of 16mm film (approximately two hours' worth) can be spliced together on one reel and the entire feature screened with no reel changes. The machine can be run from outside the projection booth (for instance, by the cashier) when wired, eliminating the need of a projectionist.

LENSES

The focal length of your lens determines how large the picture will be at a given distance (see page 99). If you are thinking of buying a machine, it is advisable to decide on a fixed place where it will be used so you can buy the lens with the correct focal length. Determine this by finding out the distance of the projector from the screen in feet and the size of the screen on which you will be projecting. Give your salesman this data, and he should be able to tell you if the standard lens of that particular model will be suitable. If it is not, then it is far cheaper to replace that lens with another of the proper focal length than to buy the projector with the incorrect lens and then buy an additional zoom lens.

However, if you are constantly changing your place of showing, consequently the picture size and projection distance, it *may* be more advantageous to spend the extra money for a zoom lens.

Since it is to your salesman's advantage to get you to buy the additional lens (more commission for him) be sure you're getting it straight.

CinemaScope films require special *anamorphic* lenses. If you are planning to screen five or more CinemaScope films within the year it may be cheaper to buy one; otherwise rent.

Even if you are not interested in purchasing a machine, the preceding pages will give you an idea of what is available for rental. The listings are by no means complete. If you desire more information, contact the main sales offices for complete brochures, as well as your local distributors of all 16mm portable projectors.

SOUND IMPROVEMENT

It is quite simple to bypass the internal amplifier in the case that you wish to maximize the clarity and volume of a particular film's sound track.

Bring the projector and its wiring diagram to a friendly retailer of amplifiers and speakers. He should easily be able to disengage the connection of the internal wires leading into the projector's internal amplifier and make a connection between those internal wires and your external amplifier. He will further be able to make an extension cord reaching from this external amplifier to the external speaker(s).

When restoring the projector to normal usage, the internal wires are simply reconnected to the internal amplifier. If you're going to take this trouble with modifying the sound, you ought to have a good speaker for it to be played through.

Chances are one of your friends has a twelve- to fifteen-inch speaker or speakers sitting in his living room that will suit your purposes. If you have a choice of speakers, ask the local sound-systems retailer which speaker will best reproduce both spoken words and music. He will need to know the wattage of your projector's amplifier, or, in case you are using an external unit, its wattage and the size of the hall. Test the modified arrangement in advance of show date.

The important thing to bear in mind is that every improvement you make in technical presentation will be felt, if not overtly noticed, by the audience. They are coming only to see the film, not the dexterity with which you dim the lights, change the reels. But these things are felt by the crowd, and you should make every attempt to have the best presentation circumstances will allow. This certainly does not mean purchasing expensive equipment; it does mean maintaining quality standards on the equipment you rent, as well as demanding excellence of your projectionist.

Putting on a film show is much more involved than it appears. Sure, anyone can rent a hall and a film and collect money. But a *real* presentation takes much thought and advance planning. The details are numerous, but the overall effect is overwhelmingly different. Transforming a drab, ordinary auditorium into a movie theater, where the film on the screen is large and bright and the sound is clear and distinct is no small feat. Yet it all can be accomplished if the group in charge is aware of all the factors that will improve the presentation.

An obvious flaw, such as an old battered screen, can be remedied as soon as surplus funds permit for an expenditure of about $125 or less.

An alert, conscientious projectionist is absolutely necessary.

Purchasing brighter wattage bulbs for use in the rental projectors may increase the brightness of the image up to 50 percent—a very considerable difference.

Audience feedback is a good way to check the society's film presentation reputation.

The manager or chairman or whoever is directly in charge of the physical running of the show should be intensely interested in the perfection of the presentation. Remember that the audience has been accustomed to regular movie theaters, where the image is large and bright, the sound is good, the seats are soft, the refreshment counter is near, and nothing is demanded of them except the price of admission. The better the presentation, the better the reputation of a society will be, and no customers will be lost as a result of technical flaws.

7

Film Source Directory

THE FILMS CITED IN THIS CHAPTER ARE GENERALLY POPULAR WITH
film societies in the United States today. Also included in the listing are
titles and references to groups of titles that will be of interest to
"specialty" groups.

Where possible the following data has been furnished for each title:
distributor; country of production; year of production; color or black-and-
white; subtitled, dubbed; running time; directors; stars.

Some titles included in this list indicate their distributor only. These
films are future 16mm releases (at the date of this writing), hence the
scanty information. The other data can be easily secured from the
distributor.

The following companies commonly distribute many of the same general
entertainment American films and are known as "general" distributors,
although many of them have "exclusives" on certain titles.

Arcus Films	Roa's Films
Budget Films	Swank Motion Pictures
Clem Williams Films	"The" Film Center
Films, Incorporated	Twyman Films
Institutional Cinema Service	Westcoast Films
Modern Sound Pictures	

While there is no assurance that any title listed here as being available from one of the above companies is also available from all the other companies, such is often the case. In any event, at least one source is listed for every film contained in this listing, and very often that distributor is the *only* source for a particular title.

DISTRIBUTOR ABBREVIATION INDEX
(Refer to Chapter 8 for addresses)

American Documentary Films	A/D
Arcus Films	ARCUS
Audio/Brandon Film Center	A/B
AVCO Embassy Pictures Corporation	AVCO
Budget Films	BUDGET
Crowell, Collier and Macmillan Films	CCM
Cinema V	CIN V
Columbia Cinematheque	COL
Contemporary Films/McGraw Hill	CON
E.Y.R. Campus Programs	EYR
"The" Film Center	"THE" F.C.
Film Images/Radim Films	F. IMAGES
Film-Makers Cooperative	FILM COOP
Films, Incorporated	FI
Genesis Films	GENESIS
William Greaves Productions	WM. GREAVES
Grove Press Film Library	GROVE
Hurlock Cine-World	HUR
Impact Films	IMPACT
Institutional Cinema Service	ICS
Ivy Films, Incorporated	IVY
Janus Films	JANUS
Leacock-Pennebaker, Incorporated	L/P
Makor Films	MAKOR
Modern Sound Pictures	MSP
National Talent Service	NTS
New Yorker Films	NEW YORKER
Newline Cinema	NEWLINE
Oberon Communications	OBERON
Pyramid Film Producers	PYRAMID
Roa's Films	ROA'S
Sherpix Films	SHERPIX

Swank Motion Pictures	SWANK
Third World Cinema Group	3rd WLD
Time/Life Films	TIME/LIFE
Twyman Films	TWYMAN
United Artists	UA 16
United Films, Incorporated	UNITED
United Productions of America	UPA
Universal Kinetic	UNIV. KIN.
Universal 16	UNIV/16
Walter Reade 16	WALTER
Warner Brothers	W/B
Westcoast Films	WESTCOAST
Clem Williams Films	CM. WMS.
Zipporah Films	ZIP

FILM TITLES

A Man for All Seasons   COL
   Gr. Br., color, 120 min.
   Dir.: Fred Zinnemann
   Star: Paul Scofield, Orson Welles, Susannah York

Abbott and Costello Features   UNITED
   USA, B/W, 74–90 min., 17 features

   The World of Abbott and Costello
   Who Done It
   Comin' Round the Mountain
   Naughty Nineties
   Abbott and Costello Meet the Keystone Cops
   Time of Their Lives
   Buck Privates
   Here Come the Coeds
   Ride 'Em Cowboy
   Abbott and Costello Meet Frankenstein
   Hold That Ghost
   Hit the Ice
   Abbott and Costello Meet the Mummy
   Keep 'Em Flying
   Little Giant
   Abbott and Costello Meet the Killer
   Buck Privates Come Home

Abbott and Costello Go to Mars   UNIV/16
Abbott and Costello In the Foreign Legion
Abbott and Costello Meet Dr. Jekyll and Mr. Hyde
Abbott and Costello Meet the Invisible Man

Jack and the Beanstalk   SWANK

Abbott and Costello Shorts
18 shorts, 10 min. each   SWANK
22 shorts, 10 min. each   MSP

Adalen 31   FI
Sweden, color, 115 min.
Dir.: Bo Widerberg
Star: Peter Schmidt, Anita Bjork

African Lion   MSP
Walt Disney Productions   FI
USA, color, 72 min.

The African Queen   SWANK
USA, 103 min.
Dir.: John Huston
Star: Humphrey Bogart, Katherine Hepburn

Airport   SWANK
USA, 1970, color 137 min.
Dir.: George Seaton
Star: Burt Lancaster, Jean Seberg, Dean Martin

A.K.A. Cassius Clay   UA/16
USA, 1970, color, 79 min.
Dir.: Jim Jacobs
Star: Muhummad Ali

Aku-Aku   CON
Sweden, 1951, color, narrated in English, 84 min.
Production and narration by Thor Heyerdahl

Al Capone   HUR
USA, 1959, B/W, 105 min.
Dir.: Richard Wilson
Star: Rod Steiger

Alex in Wonderland   FI
    USA, 1970, color, 109 min.
    Dir.: Larry Tucker, Paul Mazursky
    Star: Donald Sutherland, Federico Fellini, Jeanne Moreau

Alexander Nevsky   A/B
    USSR, 1938, B/W, subtitled, 107 min.
    Dir.: Sergei Eisenstein
    Star: Nikolai Cherkassov

Alice in Wonderland   MSP
    Animated Walt Disney Production   FI
    Based on Lewis Carroll

Alice in Wonderland   UNIV/16
    USA, B/W, 79 min.   UNITED
    W.C. Fields, Gary Cooper, Cary Grant   UNIV. KIN.

Alice's Restaurant   UA/16
    USA, 1969, color, 111 min.
    Dir.: Arthur Penn
    Star: Arlo Guthrie, James Broderick

All the Loving Couples   W/B

All Quiet on the Western Front   UNIV. KIN.
    USA, 1930, B/W, 103 min.   UNITED
    Dir.: Lewis Milestone   UNIV/16
    Star: Lew Ayres   SWANK
                                                        TWYMAN

Alphaville   CON
    France, 1965, B/W, subtitled, 100 min.
    Dir.: Jean-Luc Godard
    Star: Eddie Constantine, Anna Karina

America, America   W/B
    USA, B/W, 168 min.
    Dir.: Elia Kazan
    Star: Stathis Giallelis, Linda Marsh

America Is Hard to See   EYR
    USA, 1969, B/W, 100 min.
    Dir.: Emile de Antonio
    Star: Eugene McCarthy

The American Dreamer　　　　　　　　　　　　　　　EYR
USA, 1970, color, B/W, 100 min.
Dir.: L. M. Kit Carson
Star: Dennis Hopper

The Anderson Platoon　　　　　　　　　　　　　　　CON
France, 1966–67, B/W, English dialogue, 65 min.
Prod. and Dir.: Pierre Schoendorffel
Star: Men of 1st Platoon, B Company, 1st Cavalry
　　　　Division (Airmobile), Vietnam war documentary

The Andromeda Strain　　　　　　　　　　　　　　SWANK
USA, 1970, color, 130 min.
Dir.: Robert Wise
Star: Arthur Hill, David Wayne, James Olson

Angela: Portrait of a Revolutionary　　　　　　NEW YORKER
USA, 1970, B/W, 60 min.
Produced by Yolande Du Luart

Angels with Dirty Faces　　　　　　　　　　　　　UA/16
USA, 1938, B/W, 97 min.
Dir.: Michael Curitz
Star: James Cagney, Humphrey Bogart,
　　　　The Dead End Kids

Animal Farm　　　　　　　　　　　　　　　　　　CON
Gr. Br., 1955, color or B/W, animated, 75 min.　BUDGET
Orwell's political fable come to life

Anne of the Thousand Days　　　　　　　　　　　SWANK
USA, color, 145 min.　　　　　　　　　　　　　　CM. WMS.
Dir.: Charles Jarott　　　　　　　　　　　　　　WESTCOAST
Star: Richard Burton　　　　　　　　　　　　　　UNIV/16

Anthropology　　　　　　　　　　　　　　　　　TIME/LIFE
BBC TV/Odyssey Productions
Africa—three color films, 25 min. each
Narrated by Lowell Thomas
Asia—twelve color films, 25 min. each
Narrated by Lowell Thomas
Australian Aborigines—two color films, 25 min. each
Narrated by Lowell Thomas

Central and South America—five color films, 25 min. each
  Narrated by Lowell Thomas
Digging Up the Past—BBC TV, 20 min., B/W
Margaret Mead—BBC TV, 27 min., B/W
People Out of Time—BBC TV, 30 min., color
  (Australian aborigines)
Race to Extinction—BBC TV, 50 min., B/W
  (Mayan Indians)
The Witch Doctor—BBC TV, 35 min., B/W

Anthropology

(Complete listing of all titles available for rent and purchase in "Films for Anthropological Teaching." See bibliography for address where to obtain this manual.)

Antonio Das Mortes   GROVE
  Brazil, subtitled
  Dir.: Glauber Rocha
  Star: Maurico do Valle, Odete Lara, Othen Bastos

Arabella   UNIV/16
  Italy, color, dubbed, 91 min.
  Dir.: Mario Bolognini
  Star: Virna Lisi, Terry-Thomas, Margaret Rutherford

Arthur Penn: Themes and Variations   A/B
  USA, 1970, color, 86 min.   TIME/LIFE
  Dir.: Robert Hughes
  Star: Arthur Penn, Dede Allen, Warren Beatty, Arlo Guthrie, Dustin Hoffman

Ashes and Diamonds   JANUS
  Poland, 1958, B/W, subtitled, 105 min.
  Dir.: Andrzei Wajda

L'Avventura   JANUS
  Italy, 1960, B/W, subtitled, 145 min.
  Dir.: Michelangelo Antonioni

BBC TV Productions   TIME/LIFE

The Baby Maker   SWANK
  USA, 1970, color, 109 min.
  Dir.: James Bridges
  Star: Barbara Hershey

The Balcony   WALTER
   1963, B/W, English dialogue, 84 min.
   Adapted from Jean Genet's play
   Dir.: Joseph Strick

Ballad of a Soldier   A/B
   USSR, 1960, B/W, subtitled, 89 min.
   Dir.: Grigori Chukhrai
   Star: Vladimir Ivashor, Nikolai Kruchkov

Barbarella   FI
   France, color, English dialogue, 98 min.
   Dir.: Roger Vadim
   Star: Jane Fonda, David Hemmings

Basic Training   ZIP
   USA, 1970, B/W, 89 min.
   Dir.: Frederick Wiseman
   Stars: Draftees at Fort Knox, Kentucky

The Battle of Algiers   A/B
   Italy, 1966, B/W, subtitled, 123 min.   A/D
   Dir.: Gillo Pontecorvo
   Star: Jean Martin

Battle of Britain   UA/16
   Gr. Br., 1969, color, 132 min.
   Dir.: Guy Hamilton
   Star: Michael Caine, Laurence Olivier

Beauty and the Beast   JANUS
   France, 1946, B/W, subtitled, 90 min.
   Story, dialogue and directed by Jean Cocteau

Bed and Board   COL
   France, 1971, color, subtitled or dubbed, 97 min.
   Dir.: François Truffaut
   Star: Jean-Pierre Leaude

Belle de Jour   HUR
   French, color, subtitled or dubbed, 100 min.
   Dir.: Luis Buñuel
   Star: Catherine Deneuve

Ben-Hur   FI
  Color, 165 min.
  Dir.: William Wyler
  Star: Charlton Heston

Beneath the Planet of the Apes   FI
  USA, color, 95 min.
  Dir.: Ted Post
  Star: Charlton Heston

Bertrand Russell: Life and Times   TIME/LIFE
  Gr. Br., B/W, BBC TV, 50 min.

Betty Boop Cartoons   IVY
  B/W, 6-1/2 to 8 min.

The Bicycle Thief   A/B
  Italy, 1949, B/W, subtitled, 87 min.   NTS
  Dir.: Vittorio de Sica
  Star: Enzo Staiola

The Big Sleep   UA/16
  USA, 1946, B/W, 114 min.
  Dir.: Howard Hawks
  Star: Humphrey Bogart, Lauren Bacall

Billy Jack   W/B
  USA, 1971, color
  Dir.: T. C. Frank

Black Orpheus   JANUS
  Brazil, 1960, color, subtitled or dubbed, 103 min.
  Dir.: Marcel Camus

Black Roots   IMPACT
  USA, 1969, color, 71 min.   A/D
  Dir.: Lionel Rogosin
  Star: Flo Kennedy, Rev. Douglas Kirkpatrick

Black Views on Race   TIME/LIFE
  Twenty 4-min. films
    1. Ralph Abernathy
    2. Harry Belafonte

3. Julian Bond
4. Edward Brooke
5. H. Rap Brown
6. James Brown
7. Jim Brown
8. Stokely Carmichael
9. Shirley Chisholm
10. Muhammad Ali
11. Dick Gregory
12. Coretta King
13. Martin Luther King
14. Adam Clayton Powell
15. Jackie Robinson
16. Bayard Rustin
17. Bobby Seale
18. Carl Stokes
19. Malcolm X
20. Sidney Poitier

Blood and Sand   MSP
USA, 1922, B/W, 63 min.   SWANK
Star: Rudolph Valentino

The Blood of a Poet   A/B
France, 1930, subtitled, 55 min.
Directed and written by Jean Cocteau

Blood of the Condor   A/D
Bolivia, B/W, subtitled, 95 min.   3rd WLD
Dir.: Jorge Sanjines

Blow-Up   FI
Gr. Br., color, 108 min.
Dir.: Michelangelo Antonioni
Star: David Hemmings, Vanessa Redgrave

The Blue Angel   JANUS
Germany, 1930, B/W, subtitled, 90 min.   CON
Dir.: Josef Von Sternberg   NEW YORKER
Star: Marlene Dietrich

Blue Movie   FILM COOP
USA, color, 98 min.
Dir.: Andy Warhol

Blue Water, White Death   SWANK
  1970, color, 100 min.
  Dir.: Peter Gimbel
  Star: the great white shark

Bob and Carol and Ted and Alice   COL
  USA, 1969, color, 104 min.
  Dir.: Paul Mazursky
  Star: Natalie Wood, Robert Culp,
      Elliot Gould, Dyan Cannon

Boccaccio '70   AVCO
  Italy, 1962, color, subtitled
  Produced: Carlo Ponti
  Dir.: Vittorio De Sica, Federico Fellini, Luchino Visconti
  Star: Sophia Loren, Anita Ekberg, Romy Schneider

La Boheme   FI
  1925, silent
  Dir.: King Vidor
  Star: Lillian Gish

Le Bonheur   JANUS
  France, 1965, color, subtitled, 85 min.
  Dir.: Agnes Varda

Bonjour Tristesse   CCM
  USA, 1958, color, 94 min.   A/B
  Dir.: Otto Preminger
  Star: Jean Seberg, David Niven

Bonnie and Clyde   W/B
  USA, 1968, color
  Dir.: Arthur Penn
  Star: Faye Dunaway, Warren Beatty

Boris Karloff Horror Films   UNIV. KIN.
  10 features, USA, 1931–51, B/W, 61–92 min.

Born Free   SWANK
  Gr. Br., 1966, color, 95 min.   A/B
  Dir.: James Hill   MSP
  Star: Virginia McKenna

Borsalino   FI
  Color, 125 min.
  Dir.: Jacques Deray
  Star: Jean-Paul Belmondo, Alain Delon

The Boston Strangler   FI
  USA, color, 120 min.
  Dir.: Richard Fleischer
  Star: Tony Curtis, Henry Fonda

Le Boucher   SWANK
  France, 1971, color, subtitled
  Dir.: Claude Chabrol

Boudo Saved from Drowning   CON
  France, 1932, B/W, 87 min.
  Dir.: Jean Renoir
  Star: Michel Simon

Boy   GROVE
  Japan, color, subtitled, 97 min.
  Dir.: Nagisa Oshima
  Star: Fumio Watanabe, Tetsuo Abe, Akiko Koyama

The Boy Friend   FI
  Gr. Br., 1971, color, 109 min.
  Dir.: Ken Russell
  Star: Twiggy

A Boy Named Charlie Brown   SWANK
  USA, 1971, color, 85 min.
  Dir.: Bill Melendez
  Creator: Charles Schultz

The Boys in the Band   SWANK
  USA, 1969, color, 120 min.
  Dir.: William Friedkin
  Star: Kenneth Nelson, Leonard Frey

Brand X   NEWLINE
  Dir.: Win. Chamberlain
  Star: Taylor Mead, Abbie Hoffman

Brazil—A Report on Torture   NEW YORKER
    Chile/USA, 1971, color, subtitled, 58 min.
    Production: Saul Landau, Haskell Wexler

Breathless   CON
    France, 1959, B/W, subtitled, 89 min.
    Dir.: Jean-Luc Godard
    Star: Jean Seberg, Jean-Paul Belmondo

Brewster McCloud   FI
    USA, color, 104 min.
    Dir.: Robert Altman
    Star: Bud Cort, Sally Kellerman

The Bride Wore Black   UA/16
    France, 1968, color, subtitled, 107 min.
    Dir.: François Truffaut
    Star: Jeanne Moreau, Jean-Claude Brialy

The Bridge on the River Kwai   CON
    Gr. Br., 1957, color, 161 min.   A/B
    Dir.: David Lean   SWANK
    Star: Alec Guinness, Sessue Hayakawa   MSP
                                                       ARCUS
                                                       CM. WMS.
                                                       TWYMAN

Brotherly Love   FI
    Color, 112 min.
    Star: Peter O'Toole, Susannah York

Buck Rogers (Buster Crabbe)   IVY
    12 chapters, Serial 1936   UNITED
    (Condensed feature version:
        Destination Saturn, 100 min.)

Bugs Bunny   UA/16
    18 titles, approximately seven min. each, color

Bullitt   SWANK
    USA, 1967, color, 113 min.   W/B
    Dir.: Peter Yates   WESTCOAST
    Star: Steve McQueen

Burn!   UA/16
    Portugal, 1970, color, dubbed, 112 min.
    Dir.: Gillo Pontecorvo
    Star: Marlon Brando

Bus Stop   MSP
    USA, color, 96 min.   FI
    Star: Marilyn Monroe, Hans Conreid

Butch Cassidy and the Sundance Kid   FI
    USA, color, 112 min.
    Dir.: George Roy Hill
    Star: Paul Newman, Robert Redford, Katherine Ross

(The Making of) Butch Cassidy and the Sundance Kid   A/B
    USA, 1969, color, 52 min.
    Dir.: Robert Crawford
    Narr.: George Roy Hill
    Star: Paul Newman, Robert Redford

C.C. and Company   AVCO
    USA, 1969, color
    Dir.: Seymour Robbie
    Star: Joe Namath, Ann-Margret

The Cabinet of Dr. Caligari   JANUS
    Germany, 1919, B/W,   A/B
       silent with music score, subtitled   CON
    Dir.: Robert Wiene   NEW YORKER
    Star: Werner Krauss

Cactus Flower   COL
    USA, 1970, color, 102 min.
    Dir.: Gene Saks
    Star: Goldie Hawn, Walter Matthau, Ingrid Bergman

The Caine Mutiny   CON
    USA, 1954, color, 125 min.   A/B
    Dir.: Edward Dmytryk
    Star: Humphrey Bogart

Calcutta   EYR
    India, 1970, color, English dialogue, 115 min. PYRAMID
    Dir.: Louis Malle

Call of the Wild   FI
    From the novel by Jack London
    USA, B/W, 78 min.
    Dir.: William Wellman
    Star: Clark Gable, Loretta Young

Can Heironymus Merkin Ever Forget   UNIV. KIN.
Mercy Humppe and Find True Happiness   UNITED
    Gr. Br., 1969, color, 117 min.   UNIV/16
    Dir.: Anthony Newley
    Star: Anthony Newley, Milton Berle, George Jessel

Candy   FI
    Gr. Br., color, 122 min.
    Dir.: Christian Marquand
    Star: Ewa Aulin, Marlon Brando, Charles Aznavour,
        Ringo Starr, James Coburn, John Huston

Captain Marvel, Adventures of   IVY
    1941, serial, 12 chapters

Carnal Knowledge   AVCO
    USA, 1971, color
    Dir.: Jules Feiffer
    Star: Jack Nicholson, Arthur Garfunkel, Candice Bergen

Casablanca   CON
    USA, 1942, B/W, 102 min.   A/B
    Production: Hal Wallis   FI
    Dir.: Michael Curitz   UA/16
    Star: Humphrey Bogart, Ingrid Bergman,   CM. WMS.
        Peter Lorre, Sydney Greenstreet

The Castle   WALTER
    Adapted from a novel by Franz Kafka
    Sweden, 1968, color, 90 min.
    Dir.: Rudolph Noelte
    Star: Maximilian Schell

Castle Keep   A/B
    USA, 1969, color, 106 min.
    Dir.: Sydney Pollock
    Star: Burt Lancaster, Al Freeman, Jr.

Catch-22   FI
    USA, 1971, color, 121 min.
    Dir.: Mike Nichols
    Star: Alan Arkin, Martin Balsam,
        Richard Benjamin, Jon Voigt

Celebration at Big Sur   GENESIS
    USA, 1970, color
    Dir.: Baird Bryant, Johanna Demetrakas
    Star: Joan Baez; Crosby, Stills, Nash and Young;
        Joni Mitchell; John Sebastian

Chafed Elbows   GROVE
    USA, color and B/W, 60 min.   IMPACT
    Dir.: Robert Downey

Un Chant d'Amour   GROVE
    France, 1950, B/W, silent, 26 min.
    Dir.: Jean Genet

Charlie Chan Films   W/B
    Four features
    Castle in the Desert
    Charlie Chan at Treasure Island
    Charlie Chan in London
    Charlie Chan in Shanghai
    10 features   HUR

Charlie Chaplin, Funniest Man in the World   GROVE
    Dir.: Vernon P. Becker
    Film anthology compilation of the best of Charlie Chaplin
    Narr.: Douglas Fairbanks, Jr.

Charles Chaplin Shorts   UNIV. KIN.
    USA, B/W, silent, all approximately 13 min.   SWANK
                                                  MSP
                                                  A/B

Charlie Chaplin: Tillie's Punctured Romance   FI
    USA, 1914, B/W, silent, 40 min.
    Prod. and Dir.: Mack Sennett

Charly   FI
   USA, color, 102 min.
   Dir.: Ralph Nelson
   Star: Cliff Robertson, Claire Bloom

Chelsea Girls   FILM COOP
   Dir.: Andy Warhol
   33 min. each, total: 165 min.
   "Mario Sings"—B/W
   "Marie Menken"—color
   "Eric Tells All"—color
   "Eric and Group"—color, silent
   "Pope Ondine"—B/W
   "Nico Crying"—color

Chicago Conspiracy Circus '70   NEWLINE
   USA, 1968, color, 93 min.
   Dir.: Kerry Geltham

The Chicago Conspiracy Trial   TIME/LIFE
   USA, 1970, B/W, 180 min.
   Dir.: Christopher Burstall
   Star: Morris Carnovsky, Al Freeman, Jr., Cliff Gorman

Chicago: The Seasons Change   A/D
   USA, 1968, B/W, 45 min.
   Prod.: William Jersey, ACLU

Un Chien Andalou   JANUS
   France, 1928, B/W, music score, 16 min.   A/B
   Dir.: Luis Buñuel, Salvador Dali

Children of Paradise (L'Enfants du Paradis)   CON
   France, 1943–45, B/W, subtitled, 188 min.
   Dir.: Marcel Carne
   Star: Jean-Louis Barrault

China!   A/D
   Gr. Br., 1963, color, 65 min., English narration   IMPACT
   Dir.: Felix Greene
   91 min., color   GROVE

The China Story, One Fourth of Humanity   A/D
   Gr. Br., 1968, color, 74 min., English narration   IMPACT
   Dir.: Edgar Snow

China, Report from   F. IMAGES
   China, 1966–67, color, 90 min., English narration
   Dir.: Toshie Tokieda

Christine Jorgenson Story   UA/16
   USA, 1970, color, 89 min.
   Dir.: Irving Rapper
   Star: John Hansen

The Cincinnati Kid   FI
   USA, color, 113 min.
   Star: Steve McQueen, Edward G. Robinson, Ann-Margret

Cinema Novo Brasil   NEW YORKER
                                                  GROVE
                                                  HUR

Citizen Kane   FI
   USA, 1941, B/W, 119 min.   JANUS
   Dir.: Orson Welles   A/B
   Star: Orson Welles, Joseph Cotten

Civilization Films   TIME/LIFE
   Thirteen 52 min. color films
   Prod.: BBC
   Written and narrated by Kenneth Clark
     1. *The Frozen World*
     2. *The Great Thaw*
     3. *Romance and Reality*
     4. *Man—The Measure of All Things*
     5. *The Hero As an Artist*
     6. *Protest and Communication*
     7. *Grandeur and Obedience*
     8. *Light of Experience*
     9. *The Pursuit of Happiness*
    10. *The Smile of Reason*
    11. *The Worship of Nature*
    12. *The Fallacies of Hope*
    13. *Heroic Materialism*

Claire's Knee   COL
  France, 1971, color, subtitled or dubbed, 105 min.
  Dir.: Eric Rohmer

Closely Watched Trains   A/B
  Czechoslovakia, 1967, B/W, subtitled, 89 min.
  Dir.: Jiri Menzel

The Clowns   FI
  Italy, 1970, color, subtitled, 90 min.
  Dir.: Federico Fellini
  Star: Anita Ekberg

The Collector   COL
  Gr. Br., color, 119 min.
  Dir.: William Wyler
  Star: Terence Stamp, Samantha Eggar

Come Back, Africa   GROVE
  USA, 1959, B/W, 84 min., English dialogue   CON
  Dir.: Lionel Rogosin   A/D

Coming Apart   NEWLINE
  USA, 1968, B/W, 110 min.
  Dir.: Milton Moses Ginsberg
  Star: Rip Torn, Sally Kirkland

The Committee   A/B
  USA, 1969, color, 88 min.   UNITED
  Dir.: Del Jack   SWANK
                                                          MSP

Companeras and Companeros   NEW YORKER
  USA/Cuba, 1970, B/W, subtitled, 79 min.
  Abridged version, 45 min. available from   FILM COOP
  Prod.: Adolphas Mekas, Barbara Stone, David Stone

Compulsion   FI
  USA, B/W, 103 min.
  (Leopold-Loeb murder of 1920s)
  Star: Orson Welles, Diane Varsi

The Confession   GENESIS
   French/Italian, 1970, color, subtitled
   Dir.: Costa Gavras
   Star: Yves Montand, Simone Signoret

The Conformist   GENESIS
   Italy, 1970, color, subtitled
   Dir.: Bernardo Bertolucci
   Star: Jean-Louis Trintignant, Stefania Sandrelli

Coogan's Bluff   UNIV. KIN.
   USA, 1968, color, 100 min.   UNIV/16
   Dir.: Donald Siegel   UNITED
   Star: Clint Eastwood, Lee J. Cobb   SWANK

Cool Hand Luke   A/B
   USA, 1967, color, 129 min.   SWANK
   Dir.: Stuart Rosenberg   MSP
   Star: Paul Newman   ARCUS
                                                    BUDGET
                                                    "THE" F.C.
                                                    WESTCOAST
                                                    CM. WMS.

Copacabana   IVY
   USA, 1947, B/W
   Dir.: Alfred Green
   Star: Marx Bros., Carmen Miranda

Cotton Comes to Harlem   UA/16
   USA, 1970, color, 97 min.
   Dir.: Ossie Davis
   Star: Godfrey Cambridge

The Cousins   CON
   France, 1958, B/W, subtitled, 112 min.
   Dir.: Claude Chabrol
   Star: Jean-Claude Brialy

The Cranes Are Flying   A/B
   USSR, 1957, B/W, subtitled, 94 min.
   Dir.: Mikhail Kalatozov
   Star: Tatiana Samoilova, Alexi Batalov

The Crook   UA/16
   France, 1971, color, subtitled
   Dir.: Claude Lelouch
   Star: Jean-Louis Trintignant

Cul-de-Sac   A/B
   Gr. Br., 1966, B/W, 111 min.
   Dir.: Roman Polanski
   Star: Donald Pleasance

Curse of the Werewolf   UNIV/16
   Gr. Br., color, 91 min.
   Dir.: Terence Fisher
   Star: Oliver Reed, Anthony Dawson, Yvonne Romain

Daffy Duck   UA/16
   Seven titles, color, approximately 7 min. each

The Damned   W/B
   Italy/Gr. Br. Co-prod., 1970, color, 155 min.,
      English dialogue
   Dir.: Luchino Visconti
   Star: Dirk Bogarde, Ingrid Thulin

Dante's Inferno   TIME/LIFE
   Gr. Br., B/W, 90 min.
   Dir.: Ken Russell
   Star: Oliver Reed

Darling   A/B
   Gr. Br., 1965, B/W, 122 min.
   Dir.: John Schlesinger
   Star: Julie Christie, Dirk Bogarde

David and Lisa   WALTER
   USA, 1962, B/W, 94 min.
   Dir.: Frank Perry
   Star: Howard Da Silva, Keir Dullea, Janet Margolin

A Day at the Races   FI
   USA, B/W, 109 min.
   Dir.: Sam Wood
   Star: Groucho, Harpo, and Chico Marx,
      Maureen O'Sullivan

Day of Wrath   CON
    Denmark, 1943, B/W, subtitled, 98 min.
    Dir.: Carl Theodor Dreyer
    Star: Thorkild Roose, Lisbeth Movin

Day the Earth Caught Fire   JANUS
    England, 1962, B/W, 90 min.   A/B
    Dir.: Val Guest
    Star: Edward Tudd, Janet Munro, Leo McKern

Days of Thrills and Laughter   FI
    Star: Douglas Fairbanks, Laurel and Hardy,   MSP
        Charlie Chaplin, Mack Sennett, Boris Karloff,
        Ben Turpin, Great Houdini, Keystone Kops

Dead Birds   CON
    USA, 1963, color, English narration, 83 min.
    Dir.: Robert Gardner
    Star: W. New Guinea tribesman

Death in Venice   W/B
    Italy, 1970, color, subtitled
    Dir.: Luchino Visconti
    Star: Dirk Bogarde

The Decameron   UA/16
    Dr.: Pier Paolo Pasolini

Deep End   FI
    Poland, 1970, color, 87 min., subtitled
    Dir.: Jerzy Skolimowski
    Star: Jane Asher, John Moulder-Brown

Le Depart   CON
    Poland, 1967, B/W, subtitled, 92 min.
    Dir.: Jerzy Skolimowski
    Star: Jean-Pierre Léaud

Destry Rides Again   UNIV. KIN.
    USA, 1939, B/W, 92 min.   UNITED
    Dir.: George Marshall   SWANK
    Star: James Stewart, Marlene Dietrich   UNIV/16

The Devils   W/B
  Gr. Br., 1970, color
  Dir.: Ken Russell
  Star: Oliver Reed, Vanessa Redgrave

Diabolique   W/B
  France, B/W, subtitled, 105 min.
  Dir.: Henri-Georges Clouzot
  Star: Simone Signoret

Diary of a Mad Housewife   SWANK
  USA, 1970, color, 94 min.
  Dir.: Frank Perry
  Star: Carrie Snodgrass, Richard Benjamin

To Die in Madrid   A/B
  France, 1965, English dialogue, 90 min.
  Dir.: Frederic Rossif

Dillinger   HUR
  USA, 1944, B/W, 70 min.
  Dir.: Max Nosseck
  Star: Lawrence Tierney, Eduardo Cianelli

Dr. Jekyll and Mr. Hyde   FI
  1932
  Dir.: Robert Mamoulian

Dr. Strangelove, or How I Learned to   COL
Stop Worrying and Love the Bomb
  Gr. Br., B/W, 93 min.
  Dir.: Stanley Kubrick
  Star: Peter Sellers

La Dolce Vita   A/B
  Italy, 1961, B/W, subtitled, 180 min.
  Dir.: Federico Fellini
  Star: Marcello Mastroianni, Anouk Aimee, Anita Ekberg

Don't Look Back   L/P
  England/USA, 1965, B/W
  Dir.: Leacock/Pennebaker
  Star: Bob Dylan

Downhill Racer   FI
  USA, color, 102 min.
  Dir.: Michael Ritchie
  Star: Robert Redford

Dracula   SWANK
  1931, B/W, 75 min.   UNIV/16
  Dir.: Tod Browning
  Star: Bela Lugosi

The Dreamer   MAKOR
  Israel, 1969, color, subtitled, 87 min.

Duet for Cannibals   GROVE
  Sweden, 1968, B/W, subtitled, 105 min.
  Dir.: Susan Sontag
  Star: Adrian Asti, Lars Ekborg

Dutchman   WALTER
  Adapted from LeRoi Jones play, USA
  Star: Shirley Knight, Al Freeman, Jr.

Dynamite Chicken   EYR
  USA, 1970, color, 76 min.
  Dir.: Ernie Pintoff
  Star: Ace Trucking Company, Richard Pryor

The Earrings of Madame De . . .   CON
  France, 1953, B/W, subtitled, 105 min.
  Dir.: Max Ophuls
  Star: Charles Boyer, Vittorio De Sica

The East Is Red   CON
  China, 1965, color, 130 min.
  Prod. and film: People's Republic of China

East of Eden   A/B
  USA, 1955, color, 115 min.   SWANK
  Dir.: Elia Kazan   MSP
  Star: James Dean

8½   A/B
   Italy, 1963, B/W, dubbed or   AVCO
     subtitled, 135 min.
   Dir.: Federico Fellini
   Star: Marcello Mastroianni, Anouk Aimee

El (This Strange Passion)   A/B
   Mexico, 1952, B/W, subtitled, 82 min.
   Dir.: Luis Buñuel
   Star: Arturo de Cordova

Elvira Madigan   COL
   Sweden, 1967, color, subtitled or dubbed, 90 min.
   Dir.: Bo Widerberg
   Star: Pia Degermark, Thommy Berggren

The End of August at the Hotel Ozone   NEWLINE
   Czechoslovakia, B/W, 85 min.
   Dir.: Jan Schmidt

Endless Summer   A/B
   USA, 1966, color, 95 min.   COL
   Dir.: Bruce Brown   SWANK
   Star: Mike Hynson, Robert August   CM. WMS.
                                                     "THE" F.C.
                                                     BUDGET

Erotic Film Festival   NEWLINE
   of New York (1971) prizewinners.

Essene   ZIP
   USA, 1972, 86 min.
   Dir.: Frederick Wiseman

Esquire's First International College Film Festival   WALTER

Even Dwarfs Started Small   NEWLINE
   Germany, B/W, 110 min.
   Dir.: Werner Herzog

Exodus   UA/16
   USA, 1960, B/W, English dialogue, 207 min.
   Dir.: Otto Preminger
   Star: Paul Newman, Eva Marie Saint, Peter Lawford

Experiment in Terror   A/B
   USA, 1962, B/W, 123 min.   MSP
   Dir.: Blake Edwards
   Star: Glenn Ford, Lee Remick

The Exterminating Angel   A/B
   Mexico, 1962, B/W, subtitled, 91 min.
   Dir.: Luis Buñuel
   Star: Silvia Pinal

Eyes of Hell (3-D)   NEWLINE
   USA, B/W, 83 min.
   Dir.: Julian Roffman

Faces   WALTER
   USA, 1968, B/W, 129 min.
   Dir.: John Cassavetes
   Star: Lynn Carlin, Seymour Cassel

Fahrenheit 451   UNIV. KIN.
   France, 1966, color, subtitled, 113 min.   SWANK
   Adapted from Ray Bradbury's novel   WESTCOAST
   Dir.: François Truffaut   UNIV/16
   Star: Oskar Werner, Julie Christie   TWYMAN

Fearless Vampire Killers   FI
   USA, 1967, color, 98 min.
   Dir.: Roman Polanski
   Star: Sharon Tate

Ciao Federico (Fellini: A Director's Notebook)   A/B
(The Making of Satyricon)   NEWLINE
   1969, color, 55 min.   PYRAMID
   Dir.: Gideon Bachmann

Fellini Satyricon   UA/16
   Italy, 1970, color, subtitled, 127 min.
   Dir.: Federico Fellini

Une Femme Douce   NEW YORKER
   France, 1969, color, subtitled, 87 min.
   Dir.: Robert Bresson
   Star: Dominque Sanda

La Femme Infidèle   HUR
   France, color, subtitled, 102 min.
   Dir.: Claude Chabrol
   Star: Stephane Audran, Michel Bouquet

Fidel!   NEW YORKER
   USA/Cuba, 1969, color, 95 min.
   Dir.: Saul Landau
   Star: Castro and his Cuba, Che Guevera

W. C. Fields (Features)   UNIV. KIN.
   Eighteen features, 1932–44, B/W, 63 min.–109 min. each   UNITED
   Mrs. Wiggs of the Cabbage Patch
   Never Give a Sucker an Even Break
   The Bank Dick   SWANK
   Big Broadcast of 1938
   It's a Gift
   If I Had a Million
   Tillie and Gus
   Sensations of 1945
   Man on a Flying Trapeze
   My Little Chickadee
   Alice in Wonderland
   International House
   Mississippi
   Million Dollar Legs
   You Can't Cheat an Honest Man   SWANK
   The Old Fashioned Way
   Poppy
   Six of a Kind
   Sally of the Sawdust (1925)   SWANK

   Alice in Wonderland   WESTCOAST
   You're Telling Me
   You Can't Cheat an Honest Man
   The Bank Dick
   My Little Chickadee
   Never Give a Sucker An Even Break

W. C. Fields (Shorts)   UNITED
  USA, B/W   SWANK
  The Great Train Robbery (20 min.)   MSP
  The Fatal Glass of Beer (20 min.)
  The Barber Shop (8 min.)
  Hurry, Hurry (8 min.)
  Circus Slicker (8 min.)
  Big Thumb (8 min.)
  The Great Chase (8 min.)
  California Bound (8 min.)
  The Great McGonigle (8 min.)
  The Pharmacist (20 min.)

Fireman's Ball   CIN V
  Dir.: Milos Forman

Fires on the Plain   JANUS
  Japan, 1959, B/W, subtitled, 105 min.
  Dir.: Kon Ichikawa

The First Time   UA/16
  USA, 1969, color, 90 min.
  Dir.: James Neilson
  Star: Jacqueline Bisset

Five Summer Storied   MAC/FREE

The Fixer   FI
  Color, 132 min.
  Dir.: John Frankenheimer
  Star: Alan Bates, Dirk Bogarde

Flaming Creatures   GROVE
  USA, B/W, 60 min.
  Dir.: Jack Smith

Flash Gordon   IVY
  Star: Buster Crabbe   UNITED
  1940.
  Serial title: *Flash Gordon Conquers the Universe*
  Feature (condensed from above serial):
    Purple Death from Outer Space, 87 min.

1939.
Serial title: *Flash Gordon's Trip to Mars*
Two features from above serial (from IVY):
   1.) *Deadly Ray from Mars*, 99 min.
   2.) *Perils from the Planet Mongo*, 85 min.
Serial title: *Flash Gordon Space Soldiers*
Feature (condensed from above serial):
Spaceship to the Unknown, 95 min.

Float Like a Butterfly, Sting Like a Bee   GROVE
   USA, 1966, B/W, 94 min.
   Dir.: William Klein
   Star: Muhammad Ali/Cassius Clay

The Flower Thief   A/B
   USA, 1961, B/W, 70 min.
   Dir.: Ron Rice
   Star: Taylor Mead

The Flute and the Arrow   JANUS
   India, 1958, color, English narration, 78 min.   A/B
   Dir.: Arne Sucksdorff
   Music by Ravi Shankar

Forbidden Games   JANUS
   France, 1952, B/W, subtitled, 90 min.
   Dir.: René Clement

Fortune and Men's Eyes   FI
   USA, 1971, color, 102 min.
   Dir.: Harvey Hart
   Star: Wendall Burton, Michael Greer

Four Clowns   FI
   B/W, 97 min.
   Compilation by Robert Youngson
   Star: Stan Laurel, Oliver Hardy,
       Charley Chase, Buster Keaton

The 400 Blows   JANUS
   France, B/W, subtitled, 98 min.
   Dir.: François Truffaut
   Star: Jean-Pierre Léaude

491   JANUS
   Sweden, 1963, B/W, subtitled, 110 min.
   Dir.: Vilgot Sjoman (*I Am Curious Yellow*)

The Fox   W/B
   USA, 1966, color, 110 min.
   From D.H. Lawrence's novella
   Dir.: Mark Rydell
   Star: Sandy Dennis, Keir Dullea

Frankenstein   SWANK
   USA, 1931, B/W, 71 min.   UNIV/16
   Dir.: James Whale
   Star: Boris Karloff

Freaks   A/B
   USA, 1932, B/W, 61 min.
   Dir.: Tod Browning

Frenzy   SWANK
   Gr. Br., 1971, color, 116 min.
   Dir.: Alfred Hitchcock
   Star: Jon Finch, Barry Foster

From Here to Eternity   A/B
   USA, 1953, B/W, 118 min.
   Dir.: Fred Zinnemann
   Star: Burt Lancaster, Deborah Kerr,
         Montgomery Clift, Frank Sinatra

Fu Manchu, Face of   MSP
   B/W
   Star: Nigel Green, Tsai Chin

Fu Manchu, Mask of   FI
   1931
   Dir.: Charles Brabin

G-Men   UA/16
   USA, 1935, B/W, 85 min.
   Dir.: William Keighley
   Star: James Cagney

The Garden of the Finzi Continis   CIN V
   Dir.: Luchino Visconti

Gate of Hell   SWANK
   Japan, 1956, B/W, subtitled   TWYMAN
   Dir.: Teinoske Kinugasa
   Star: Machiko Kyo, Hazuo Hasegawa

The General   SWANK
   USA, 1926, B/W, silent, 90 min.
   Star: Buster Keaton

Genesis I, II, III, IV   GENESIS
   Each a compilation of contemporary independent
   film-makers' shorts.

Gentlemen Prefer Blondes   FI
   USA, 1953, color, 91 min.
   Dir.: Howard Hawks
   Star: Marilyn Monroe, Jane Russell, Charles Coburn

Georgy Girl   SWANK
   Gr. Br., 1966, B/W, 100 min.   A/B
   Dir.: Silvio Narizzano   ARCUS
   Star: Lynn Redgrave, Alan Bates   CM. WMS.
                                                        WESTCOAST
                                                        BUDGET

Gertrud   CON
   Denmark, 1964, B/W, subtitled, 115 min.
   Dir.: Carl Dreyer
   Star: Nina Pens Rode, Bendt Rothe, Ebbe Rode

Gervaise   WALTER
   France, 1957, B/W, subtitled, 116 min.
   Dir.: René Clement
   Star: Françoise Perier, Maria Schell

Gimme Shelter   CIN V
   USA, color
   Dir.: Maysles Brothers
   Star: Rolling Stones, Tina Turner

The Gladiators   NEWLINE
    Sweden, color, 90 min.
    Dir.: Peter Watkins

Glen and Randa   W/B
    USA, 1971, color
    Dir.: Jim McBride

The Gold Rush   CON
    USA, 1925, B/W, with new music score, 85 min.   BUDGET
    Written, produced, starred and directed by   JANUS
        Charlie Chaplin   A/B

Golden Age of Comedy   MSP
    Star: Laurel and Hardy, Will Rogers,   CM. WMS.
        Jean Harlow, Ben Turpin,   FI
        Harry Langdon, and others   "THE" F.C.
                                                                   BUDGET

Miss Goodall and the Wild Chimpanzees   FI
    Gr. Br., color, 51 min.
    National Geographic Society

Goodbye, Columbus   FI
    USA, color, 105 min.
    Dir.: Larry Peerce
    Star: Richard Benjamin, Ali MacGraw

Goodbye, Mr. Chips   FI
    Gr. Br., color, 151 min.
    Dir.: Herbert Ross
    Star: Peter O'Toole, Petula Clark, Michael Redgrave

The Gospel According to St. Matthew   A/B
    Italy, 1964, B/W, subtitled or dubbed   WALTER
    Dir.: Pier Paolo Pasolini   (35MM ONLY)
    Star: Margherita Caruso, Enrique Irazoqui

The Graduate   AVCO
    USA, color
    Dir.: Mike Nichols
    Star: Dustin Hoffman, Anne Bancroft, Katherine Ross

Grand Illusion   JANUS
    France, 1937, B/W, subtitled, 111 min.
    Dir.: Jean Renoir

The Great British Train Robbery   W/B

The Great Dictator   IVY
    Star: Charlie Chaplin

Great Expectations   UNIV/16
    1934, B/W, 100 min.
    Dir.: Stuart Walker
    Star: Jane Wyatt, Phillips Holmes,
        Henry Hill, Francis L. Sullivan

Great Expectations   WALTER
    Gr. Br., 1947, B/W, 115 min.
    Dir.: David Lean
    Star: John Mills, Jean Simmons

The Great Wall of China   GROVE
    B/W, 92 min.
    Dir.: Joel Tuber

The Great White Hope   FI
    USA, 1971, color, 103 min.
    Dir.: Martin Ritt
    Star: James Earl Jones, Jane Alexander

The Greatest Story Ever Told   UA/16
    USA, 1965, color, 141 min.
    Dir.: George Stevens
    Star: Max Von Sydow, Carroll Baker,
        Pat Boone, Jose Ferrer, Van Heflin,
        Charlton Heston, Angela Lansbury

Greed   FI
    1923, silent
    Dir.: Eric Von Stroheim
    Star: Zasu Pitts, Jean Hersholt

Groove Tube Series   NTS
    Videotape programs

Groupies   NEWLINE
   USA, color, 88 min.
   Dir.: Ron Dorfman

La Guerre Est Finie   A/B
   France, 1966, subtitled, 121 min.
   Dir.: Alain Resnais
   Star: Yves Montand

Guess Who's Coming to Dinner?   COL
   USA, color, 108 min.   SWANK
   Dir.: Stanley Kramer   WESTCOAST
   Star: Katherine Hepburn, Spencer Tracy, Sidney Poitier

Gunga Din   JANUS
   USA, 1939, B/W, 107 min.   FI
   Dir.: George Stevens
   Star: Cary Grant, Douglas Fairbanks, Jr.,
      Sam Jaffee, Joan Fontaine

The Guns of Navarone   SWANK
   USA, 1961, color, 157 min.   A/B
   Dir.: J. Lee Thompson   MSP
   Star: Gregory Peck, David Niven, Anthony Quinn

Hamlet   COL
   Gr. Br., color, 114 min.
   Dir.: Tony Richardson
   Star: Marianne Faithfull, Nicol Williamson

Hamlet   WALTER
   Gr. Br., 1950, B/W, 152 min.
   Dir.: Laurence Olivier
   Star: Laurence Olivier, Jean Simmons, Peter Cushing

Hamlet   UA/16
   Russia, 1966, B/W, subtitled, 148 min.
   Dir.: Grigory Kozintsev
   Star: Innokenti Smoktunovsky, Anastasia Vertinskaya

A Hard Day's Night   UA/16
   Gr. Br., 1964, B/W, 90 min.
   Dir.: Richard Lester
   Star: the Beatles

The Harder They Fall   MSP
    USA, 1956, B/W, 109 min.   A/B
    Dir.: Mark Robson
    Star: Humphrey Bogart, Rod Steiger

Au Hasard Balthazar   NEWLINE
    France, B/W, 96 min.
    Dir.: Robert Bresson

He Walked Through the Fields   MAKOR
    Israel, B/W, subtitled, 90 min.
    Star: Assaf Dayan

Hello Dolly   FI
    USA, 1970, color, 148 min.
    Dir.: Gene Kelly
    Star: Barbra Streisand, Walter Matthau

The Hellstrom Chronicle   CIN V

Help!   UA/16
    Gr. Br., 1965, color, 90 min.
    Dir.: Richard Lester
    Star: the Beatles

Hendrix at Berkeley   AM.
    USA, 1970, color, 50 min.   ENT.
    Star: Jimi Hendrix, Mitch Mitchell, Billy Cox   ASSOC. INC.

Henry V   WALTER
    Gr. Br., 1946, color, 137 min.
    Dir.: Laurence Olivier
    Star: Laurence Olivier, Renee Asherson, Leo Genn

High School   ZIP
    USA, 1967, B/W, 75 min.
    Dir.: Frederick Wiseman

The Hired Hand   SWANK
    USA, 1971, color, 102 min.
    Star: Peter Fonda

Hiroshima, Mon Amour   A/B
   France, 1959, B/W, subtitled, 88 min.   CON
   Dir.: Alain Resnais
   Star: Emmanuelle Riva, Eiji Okada

Hiroshima/Nagasaki   A/D
   1945 atom bombings, filmed by Japanese camera
      teams, available to public only since 1970

The Holy Outlaw   NEW YORKER
   USA, 1970, B/W, 59 min.
   Prod. and Dir.: Lee Lockwood, Don Lenzer

Hopalong Cassidy Series   UNITED
   USA, B/W, 64-68 min., 6 features

The Horror Chamber of Doctor Faustus   UA/16
   France, 1962, B/W, 95 min.
   Dir.: Georges Franju
   Star: Pierre Brasseur

Hospital   ZIP
   USA, 1967, B/W, 84 min.
   Dir.: Frederick Wiseman

The Hour of the Furnaces   3rd WLD
   Argentina
   Authors: Octavio Getino, Fernando Solanas

   Three parts, total 4 hours and 20 min.

   Part I—*Neocolonialism and Violence*
   (Argentina, B/W, subtitled, 95 min.)

   Part II—*Act of Liberation*
   (Argentina, B/W, subtitled, 120 min.)

   Part III—*Violence and Liberation*
   (Argentina, B/W, subtitled, 45 min.)

Hour of the Wolf   UA/16
   Sweden, 1968, B/W, subtitled, 88 min.
   Dir.: Ingmar Bergman
   Star: Liv Ullmann, Max Von Sydow

How I Won the War   UA/16
   Gr. Br., 1967, B/W, 111 min.
   Dir.: Richard Lester
   Star: John Lennon

Adventures of Huckleberry Finn   FI
   USA, B/W, 91 min.
   Star: Mickey Rooney

Huey!   A/D
   USA, 1968, B/W, 33 min.
   Black Panther party rally, Oakland

The Hunchback of Notre Dame   A/B
   Victor Hugo's classic   FI
   USA, 1922, B/W, silent, 105 min.   UNITED
   Dir.: Wallace Worsley   SWANK
   Star: Lon Chaney   F. IMAGES

Hunger in America   A/D
   USA, 1968, B/W, 54 min.
   CBS News documentary

The Hunters Are the Hunted   F. IMAGES
   Germany, 1969, subtitled, 84 min.
   Dir.: Peter Fleischmann
   Star: Martin Speer, Angela Winkler

Husbands   COL
   USA, 1970, color, 142 min.
   Dir.: John Cassavetes
   Star: Ben Gazzara, Peter Falk, John Cassavetes

The Hustler   FI
   USA, B/W, 135 min.
   Dir.: Robert Rossen
   Star: Paul Newman, Jackie Gleason,
       Piper Laurie, George C. Scott

I Am Curious (Yellow), 120 min.   GROVE
I Am Curious (Blue), 110 min.
   Sweden, B/W, subtitled and dubbed
   Dir.: Vilgot Sjoman
   Star: Lena Nyman

I Love You, Alice B. Toklas   A/B
    USA, 1968, color, 93 min.   SWANK
    Dir.: Hy Averback   MSP
    Star: Peter Sellers, Leigh Taylor-Young   WESTCOAST
                                                           BUDGET

I Never Sang for My Father   COL
    USA, 1970, color, 93 min.
    Dir.: Gilbert Cates
    Star: Gene Hackman, Estelle Parsons, Melvyn Douglas

I Want What I Want   SWANK
    USA, 1972, color, 91 min.
    Dir.: John Dexter
    Star: Anne Heywood

Ice   NEW YORKER
    USA, 1969, B/W, 132 min.   FILM COOP
    Dir.: Robert Kramer

Ichabod and Mister Toad   MSP
    Walt Disney Production   FI
    Based on "The Legend of Sleepy Hollow"
      by Washington Irving
    Animated, color, 68 min.

If . . .   FI
    Gr. Br., color, 111 min.
    Dir.: Lindsay Anderson
    Star: Malcolm McDowell, Sean Bury

Ikiru (To Live)   A/B
    Japan, 1952, B/W, subtitled, 140 min.
    Dir.: Akira Kurosawa
    Star: Takashi Shimura

The Illustrated Man   W/B
    Gr. Br., 1964, color, 103 min.
    Dir.: Jack Smigut
    Star: Rod Steiger, Claire Bloom
    From Ray Bradbury's novel

In Cold Blood   COL
   Gr. Br., B/W, 133 min.
   Dir.: Richard Brooks

In the Company of Men   WM. GREAVES
   USA, 1969, B/W, 52 min.
   Dir.: William Greaves

In the Year of the Pig   CON
   USA, 1968, B/W, 100 min.   NEW YORKER
   Dir.: Emile de Antonio   (35MM)
   Academy Award, Best Documentary   A/D

The Incredible Shrinking Man   SWANK
   USA, B/W, 94 min.   UNIV/16
   Star: Grant Williams, Randy Stuart

Inside North Vietnam   GROVE
   Color, 91 min.   IMPACT
   Dir.: Felix Greene   A/D

Interlude   A/B
   Gr. Br., 1968, color, 113 min.
   Dir.: Kevin Billington
   Star: Oskar Werner, Donald Sutherland

Interviews with My Lai Veterans   WALTER
   USA, 1970, color, 22 min.   NEW YORKER
   Dir.: Joseph Strick   GROVE
   Photog,: Haskell Wexler

Intolerance   FI (HAND-
   USA, 1916, B/W, silent, 121 min.   TINTED VERSION)
   Dir.: D.W. Griffith   A/B
   Star: Lillian Gish

Invasion of the Body Snatchers   IVY
   USA, 1956, B/W, 80 min.
   Dir.: Don Siegel
   Star: Kevin McCarthy, Dana Wynter

Investigation of a Citizen Above Suspicion   COL
    Italy, 1970, color, subtitled or dubbed, 114 min.

Invisible Man   UNIV/16
    Gr. Br., B/W, 72 min.
    Dir.: James Whale
    Star: Claude Rains, Gloria Stuart

It's a Mad, Mad, Mad, Mad World   UA/16
    USA, color

The Italian Straw Hat   CON
    France, 1927, B/W, silent, English titles,
      added music score, 76 min.
    Dir.: René Clair
    Star: Alice Tissot, Albert Prejean

Ivan the Terrible (Part I), 1944, 96 min.   A/B
Ivan the Terrible (Part II), 1946, 90 min.
    USSR, B/W, subtitled
    Dir.: Sergei Eisenstein
    Star: Nikolai Cherkassov

Jailhouse Rock   FI
    USA, B/W, 96 min.
    Star: Elvis Presley

Jane (Fonda)   TIME/LIFE
    USA, B/W, 54 min.
    Her Broadway debut

Joe   W/B
    USA, 1969, color, 107 min.
    Star: Peter Boyle

Joe Hill   FI
    Sweden, 1970, color, subtitled, 114 min.
    Dir.: Bo Widerberg
    Star: Thommy Berggren

John and Yoko, Films of   GENESIS
    1967–70, shorts
    Compilation program

Johnny Got His Gun   W/B
    USA, 1971, color
    Dir.: Dalton Trumbo

Jules and Jim   JANUS
    France, 1961, B/W, subtitled, 104 min.
    Dir.: François Truffaut
    Star: Jeanne Moreau, Oskar Werner

Juliet of the Spirits   A/B
    Italy, 1965, B/W, subtitled, 137 min.
    Dir.: Federico Fellini
    Star: Giulietta Masina

Buster Keaton Shorts   A/B
    Seventeen titles produced from 1920–23,
        from 17 to 23 min. each
    USA, B/W, silent

Key Largo   CON
    USA, 1948, B/W, 101 min.   A/B
    Dir.: John Huston   UA/16
    Star: Humphrey Bogart, Edward G. Robinson,
        Lauren Bacall

The Keystone Cops   SWANK
    Good Old Corn
    Wife and Auto Trouble
    Keystone Hotel
    Desperate Scoundrel

Kidnapped   FI
    Walt Disney Production
    From novel by Robert Louis Stevenson
    USA, color, 94 min.
    Star: Peter Finch, Peter O'Toole

The Killing of Sister George   FI
    Gr. Br., color, 138 min.
    Dir.: Robert Aldrich
    Star: Susannah York, Beryl Reid, Coral Browne

King and Country   A/B
Gr. Br., 1964, B/W, 86 min.
Dir.: Joseph Losey
Star: Dirk Bogarde, Tom Courtenay

King Kong   FI
Star: Fay Wray

King Kong   JANUS
USA, 1933, B/W, 105 min.
Prod.: David O. Selznick

King of Hearts   UA/16
France, 1967, color, subtitled, 101 min.
Dir.: Philippe de Broca
Star: Alan Bates

King Murray   EYR
USA, 1970, color, 80 min.
Dir.: David Hoffman
Star: Murray

King Rat   CON
USA, 1965, B/W, 134 min.   A/B
Dir.: Bryan Forbes   WESTCOAST
Star: George Segal

Klute   W/B
USA, 1971, color
Dir.: Alan J. Pakula
Star: Jane Fonda, Donald Sutherland

Knife in the Water   JANUS
Poland, 1962, B/W, subtitled, 94 min.
Dir.: Roman Polanski

Kon-Tiki   CON
Sweden, 1947, B/W, English narration, 75 min.
Prod.: Artfilm, Sweden
Photog. and Narr.: Thor Heyerdahl

Kwaidan   WALTER
Japan, 1965, B/W, subtitled
Horror anthology

The L-Shaped Room   COL
   Gr. Br., B/W, 124 min.
   Dir.: Bryan Forbes
   Star: Leslie Caron

Lady Chatterley's Lover   A/B
   France, 1955, B/W, subtitled, 102 min.

The Landlord   UA/16
   USA, 1970, color, 113 min.
   Dir.: Hal Ashby
   Star: Beau Bridges, Lee Grant, Pearl Bailey

Harry Langdon Films   A/B
   Eleven features, circa 1926–33

The Last Movie   SWANK
   USA, color, 108 min.
   Dir. and Star: Dennis Hopper

Last Summer   HUR
   USA, 1969, color, 97 min.
   Dir.: Frank Perry
   Star: Barbara Hershey

Last Year at Marienbad   A/B
   France, 1961, B/W, subtitled, 93 min.
   Dir.: Alain Resnais
   Star: Delphine Seyrig

Laurel and Hardy Features and Shorts   FI
   Eight features, 66 to 69 min.
   Eight shorts (silent), 21 to 25 min., 1927–29
   All produced by Hal Roach
   Sixteen features   MSP
   Eight featurettes (30 min. each)
   Fourteen silent shorts (20 min. each)
      (produced 1927–29)
   Twelve features   WESTCOAST
   Sound and silent shorts

Laurel and Hardy   A/B
   USA, 1927–32, B/W, silent   W/B
   Sixteen shorts, all about 20 min.   UNITED

Three features   SWANK
Twenty-three shorts
Thirty-seven shorts and featurettes

The Lavender Hill Mob   CON
    Gr. Br., 1951, B/W, 80 min.   JANUS
    Dir.: Charles Crichton   SWANK
    Star: Alec Guinness

Law and Order   ZIP
    USA, 1968, B/W, 81 min.
    Dir.: Frederick Wiseman

Le Mans   SWANK
    USA, 1970, 106 min.
    Dir.: Lee H. Katzin
    Star: Steve McQueen

The Leather Boys   A/B
    Gr. Br., 1963, B/W, 103 min.
    Dir.: Sidney J. Furie
    Star: Rita Tushingham

Lenny Bruce/Without Tears   NEW YORKER
    USA, 1971, B/W, 85 min.
    Dir. and Prod.: Fred Baker
    Star: Lenny Bruce

Lenny Bruce on TV   NEW YORKER
    USA, 1971, B/W, 35 min.
    Kinescopes of two Steven Allen
       shows (1959) and one unaired TV pilot (1961).

The Life of O-Haru   NEW YORKER
    Japan, 1952, B/W, subtitled, 133 min.
    Dir.: Kenji Mizoguchi
    Star: Kinuyo Tanaka, Toshiro Mifune

The Lion in Winter   AVCO
    USA, color, 134 min.
    Dir.: Anthony Harvey
    Star: Peter O'Toole, Katherine Hepburn

Lions Love   EYR
    USA, 1970, color, 110 min.
    Dir.: Agnes Varda
    Star: Viva, Ragni and Rado

Little Big Man   SWANK
    USA, 1970, color, 139 min.
    Dir.: Arthur Penn
    Star: Dustin Hoffman, Faye Dunaway,
        Chief Dan George, Martin Balsam

Little Caesar   CON
    USA, 1930, B/W, 77 min.   A/B
    Dir.: Mervyn LeRoy   UA/16
    Star: Edward G. Robinson, Douglas Fairbanks, Jr.

Little Fauss and Big Halsey   FI
    USA, 1970, color, 97 min.
    Dir.: Sidney Furie
    Star: Robert Redford, Michael J. Pollard

Little Murders   GENESIS
    USA, 1970, color
    Dir.: Alan Arkin
    Star: Donald Sutherland, Lou Jacobi

Lola Montès   A/B
    France, 1955, color, subtitled, 110 min.
    Dir.: Max Ophuls
    Star: Peter Ustinov, Oskar Werner

The Loneliness of the Long Distance Runner   WALTER
    Gr. Br., 1962, B/W, 103 min.
    Dir.: Tony Richardson
    Star: Tom Courtenay, Michael Redgrave

Lonesome Cowboys   FILM COOP
    USA, color, 116 min.
    Andy Warhol western
    Star: Viva, Taylor Meade

Long Ago, Tomorrow   CIN V

Long Day's Journey into Night   A/B
    USA, 1962, B/W, 136 min.   UNITED
    Dir.: Sidney Lumet
    Star: Katherine Hepburn, Ralph Richardson, Jason Robards

Lord of the Flies   WALTER
    Gr. Br., 1963, B/W, 90 min.
    Dir.: Peter Brook
    Star: James Aubrey, Tom Chapin, Hugh Edwards

The Lone Ranger and the Lost City of Gold   UNITED
    USA, color, 80 min.
    Star: Clayton Moore, Jay Silverheels

Love Affair, or the Case of the Missing Switchboard Operator A/B
    (An affair of the heart)
    Yugoslavia, 1967, B/W, subtitled, 70 min.
    Dir.: Dusan Makavejev
    Star: Eva Ras

The Love Game   CON
    France, 1960, B/W, subtitled, 85 min.
    Dir.: Philippe de Broca
    Star: Jean-Pierre Cassel, Genevieve Cluny

Love Story   FI
    USA, 1971, color, 99 min.
    Dir.: Arthur Hiller
    Star: Ali MacGraw, Ryan O'Neal

Love with the Proper Stranger   FI
    USA, B/W, 100 min.
    Star: Steve McQueen, Natalie Wood

The Loved One   FI
    USA, B/W, 116 min.
    Dir.: Tony Richardson
    Star: Jonathan Winters

Loves of a Blonde   A/B
    Czechoslovakia, 1965, B/W, subtitled, 88 min.
    Dir.: Milos Forman
    Star: Hana Brejchova

The Loves of Isadora   UNIV. KIN.
    Gr. Br., 1969, color, 131 min.   UNITED
    Dir.: Karel Reisz   SWANK
    Star: Vanessa Redgrave, Jason Robards   UNIV/16

Luminous Procuress   GROVE
    USA, 1971
    Dir.: Steven Arnold
    Star: Pandora, The Cockettes

Lupo   MAKOR
    Israel, color, English track, 100 min.

M   JANUS
    Germany, 1930, B/W, subtitled, 99 min.   A/B
    Dir.: Fritz Lang
    Star: Peter Lorre

M*A*S*H   FI
    USA, color, 113 min.
    Dir.: Robert Altman
    Star: Donald Sutherland, Elliott Gould, Sally Kellerman

Ma and Pa Kettle Features   UNITED
    Seven features, 74 to 82 min.   UNIV/16
    Star: Marjorie Main, Percy Kilbride

Macunaima   NEWLINE
    Brazil, color, 92 min.
    Dir.: Joaquin Pedro de Andrade

The Magic Christian   WESTCOAST
    Gr. Br., 1969, color, 95 min.
    Dir.: Joseph McGrath
    Star: Peter Sellers, Ringo Starr

Magic Garden of Stanley Sweetheart   FI
    USA, 1970, color, 117 min.
    Dir.: Leonard Horn
    Star: Michael Greer

The Maltese Falcon   CON
    USA, 1941, B/W, 100 min.   A/B
    Dir.: John Huston   FI
    Star: Peter Lorre, Sydney Greenstreet, Humphrey Bogart   UA/16

A Man and A Woman   HUR
  France, color, subtitled or dubbed, 102 min.
  Dir.: Claude Lelouch

A Man Called Horse   SWANK
  USA, 1970, color, 114 min.
  Dir.: Elliot Silverstein
  Star: Richard Harris, Dame Judith Andersen

A Man Escaped   CON
  France, 1956, B/W, subtitled, 94 min.
  Dir.: Robert Bresson
  Star: François Leterrier, Charles LeClainche

Marat Sade   UA/16
  Gr. Br., 1967, color, 115 min.
  Dir.: Peter Brook
  Star: Patrick Magee, Glenda Jackson

Martin Luther King   TIME/LIFE
  Gr. Br., B/W, 30 min.

Martin Luther King: The Man and the March   A/D
  USA, 1968, B/W, 59 min.

Marx Brothers Features   UNIV. KIN.
  USA   UNITED
  Coconuts, 1929, 96 min., B/W   WESTCOAST
  Duck Soup, 1933, 72 min., B/W
  Monkey Business, 1931, 81 min., B/W
  Horse Feathers, 70 min., B/W

Masculine/Feminine   COL
  France, B/W, subtitled, 103 min.
  Dir.: Jean-Luc Godard
  Star: Jean-Pierre Léaude

McCabe & Mrs. Miller   W/B
  USA, 1971, color
  Dir.: Robert Altman
  Star: Warren Beatty, Julie Christie

Me and My Brother   NEW YORKER
  USA, 1968, color or B/W, 91 min.
  Dir.: Robert Frank
  Star: Allen Ginsberg, Julius Orlovsky

Medea   NEWLINE
  Italy, color, 110 min.
  Dir.: Pier Paolo Pasolini
  Star: Maria Callas

Medicine Ball Caravan   W/B
  USA, 1971, color
  Dir.: François Reichenbach

Medium Cool   FI
  USA, color, 110 min.
  Dir.: Haskell Wexler
  Star: Chicago Democratic Convention (1968)

Mein Kampf   MSP
  Sweden, 1961, B/W, English narration, 119 min.   CON
  Prod.: T. Sjoberg   A/B
  Documentary of the origin, ascendancy and
    destruction of Adolf Hitler and the Third Reich

Mephisto Waltz   FI
  USA, 1971, color, 108 min.
  Dir.: Paul Wendkos
  Star: Alan Alda, Jacqueline Bisset, Barbara Parkins

Metropolis   FI
  Germany, 1927, B/W, silent, English titles, 93 min.   A/B
  Dir.: Fritz Lang   UNITED
  Star: Brigitte Helm, Gustane Froelich

Mexican Bus Ride   SWANK
  Mexico, 1951, B/W, subtitled, 73 min.   CON
  Dir.: Luis Buñuel   TWYMAN
  Grand Prize, D'Avant-Garde at Cannes

Mickey One   MSP
   USA, 1965, B/W, 93 min.   A/B
   Dir.: Arthur Penn   ARCUS
   Star: Warren Beatty, Franchot Tone

Midnight Cowboy   UA/16
   USA, 1969, color, 113 min.
   Dir.: John Schlesinger
   Star: Dustin Hoffman, Jon Voigt

Millhouse: A White Comedy   NEW YORKER
   USA, 1970, 92 min.
   Dir.: Emile de Antonio

Le Million   A/B
   France, 1931, B/W, subtitled, 80 min.
   Dir.: René Clair
   Star: Rene Lefevre, Annabella, Paul Olivier

Minnie and Moskowitz   SWANK
   USA, 1971, color, 114 min.
   Dir.: John Cassavetes
   Star: Gena Rowlands, Seymour Cassel

Mississippi Mermaid   UA/16
   France, 1969, color, subtitled, 110 min.
   Dir.: François Truffaut
   Star: Catherine Deneuve, Jean-Paul Belmondo

Mister Freedom   GROVE
   France, 1967, color, English dialogue, 95 min.
   Dir.: William Klein
   Star: Donald Pleasance, Delphine Seyrig

Mondo Cane   A/B
   Italy, 1962, color, English narration, 105 min.
   Dir.: Gualtiero Jacopetti

Monkey Business   SWANK
   USA, B/W, 70 min.
   Star: Marx Brothers

Monterey Pop   L/P
   USA, 1967, color, 75 min.
   Dir.: Leacock/Pennebaker
   Star: Janis Joplin, Jimi Hendrix, Otis Redding

Morgan!   COL
   Gr. Br., B/W, 97 min.
   Dir.: Karel Reisz
   Star: Vanessa Redgrave, David Warner

Morocco   UNIV. KIN.
   USA, 1930, B/W, 97 min.   UNITED
   Dir.: Josef von Sternberg   UNIV/16
   Star: Gary Cooper, Marlene Dietrich, Adolphe Menjou   TWYMAN

The Mouse That Roared   CON
   Gr. Br., 1959, color, 83 min.   A/B
   Dir.: Jack Arnold   ARCUS ı
   Star: Peter Sellers, Jean Seberg   CM. WMS.

The Mummy   SWANK
   B/W, 88 min.   UNIV/16
   Dir.: Karl Laemmle
   Star: Boris Karloff

The Murder of Fred Hampton   NTS
   USA, 1970, B/W, 88 min.
   Dir.: Mike Gray

Mutiny on the Bounty   FI
   Gr. Br., 1935, B/W, 132 min.
   Star: Charles Laughton, Clark Gable, Franchot Tone

My Life to Live   CON
   France, 1962, B/W, subtitled, 82 min.
   Dir.: Jean-Luc Godard
   Star: Anna Karina, André Labarthe

My Night at Maud's   CON
(Ma Nuit Chez Maud)
   France, 1969, 109 min.
   Dir.: Eric Rohmer
   Star: Jean-Louis Trintignant, Françoise Fabian

My Sister, My Love   A/B
  Sweden, 1967, B/W, subtitled, 97 min.
  Dir.: Vilgot Sjoman
  Star: Bibi Andersson

Myra Breckenridge   FI
  USA, 1970, color, 94 min.
  Dir.: Michael Sarne
  Star: Raquel Welch, Mae West, John Huston, Rex Reed

Nanook of the North   CON
  USA, 1920–21, B/W, silent, 55 min.
  Dir.: Robert Flaherty

Ned Kelly   UA/16
  USA, 1970, color, 103 min.
  Dir.: Tony Richardson
  Star: Mick Jagger

Negatives   WALTER
  Gr. Br., color, feature
  Dir.: Peter Medak
  Star: Glenda Jackson, Diane Cilento

Newsreels   UA/16
  1906–47
  Sixty newsreel compilations, approximately 12 min. each

A Night at the Opera   FI
  USA, B/W, 93 min.
  Dir.: Sam Wood
  Star: Groucho, Harpo, and Chico Marx

Night of the Living Dead   WALTER
  USA, 1968, B/W, 90 min.
  Dir.: George A. Romero
  Star: Duane Jones, Judith O'Dea

1984   A/B
  Based on the novel by George Orwell
  Dir.: Michael Anderson
  Star: Edmond O'Brien, Michael Redgrave

1985   CCM
  USA, color, 56 min.
  Fictionalized eco-catastrophe newscast produced by
    professional newsmen
  Star: Vernon Hixson, Russ Degal, Joe Nagy, Lenny
      Blondheim, Larry Cazaran, Zen Putterman

Nixon's Checkers Speech   NEW YORKER
  USA, 1952, B/W, 30 min.
  Prod.: David Loeb Weiss

No Blade of Grass   FI
  Gr. Br., color, 97 min.
  Dir.: Cornel Wilde
  Star: Nigel Davenport, Anthony May

No Vietnamese Ever Called Me Nigger   A/D
  USA, 1968, B/W, 68 min.

Nothing but a Man   A/B
  USA, 1964, B/W, 92 min.   A/D
  Dir.: Michael Roemer
  Star: Ivan Dixon, Abby Lincoln

La Notte   UA/16
  Italy, 1961, B/W, subtitled, 120 min.
  Dir.: Michelangelo Antonioni
  Star: Jeanne Moreau, Marcello Mastroianni, Monica Vitti

A Nous La Liberté   CON
  France, 1931, B/W, subtitled, 87 min.
  Dir.: René Clair
  Star: Raymond Cordy, Henri Marchand

Nude Restaurant   FILM COOP
  USA, color, 95 min.
  Dir.: Andy Warhol
  Star: Viva, Taylor Meade

The Nun   A/B
  France, 1965, color, subtitled, 130 min.
  Dir.: Jacques Rivette
  Star: Anna Karina

Oedipus Rex   CON
   Canada, 1956, color, 90 min.
   Dir.: Tyrone Guthrie
   Star: Stratford, Ontario, Shakespearean Festival players

Of Human Bondage   NEW YORKER
   USA, 1934, B/W, 83 min.
   Dir.: John Cromwell
   Star: Bette Davis, Leslie Howard

Oliver!   COL
   Gr. Br., 1968, color, 153 min.
   Dir.: Sir Carol Reed
   Star: Ron Moody, Jack Wild, Mark Lester

The Omega Man   W/B
   Star: Charlton Heston

On Any Sunday   CIN V
   Dir.: Bruce Brown

On the Bowery   CON
   USA, 1956, B/W, 65 min.   GROVE
   Dir.: Lionel Rogosin   IMPACT

On the Waterfront   MSP
   USA, 1954, B/W, 108 min.   CON
   Dir.: Elia Kazan   A/B
   Star: Marlon Brando, Rod Steiger, Eva Marie Saint   SWANK
                                                        ARCUS
                                                        CM. WMS.
                                                        WESTCOAST
                                                        BUDGET

One Day in the Life of Ivan Denisovich   SWANK
   Gr. Br., 1971, color, 100 min.
   Dir.: Casper Wrede
   Star: Tom Courtenay

Open City   CON
   Italy, 1945, B/W, subtitled, 103 min.
   Dir.: Roberto Rossellini
   Star: Anna Magnani, Aldo Fabrizi

Orphans of the Storm   A/B
   USA, 1921, B/W, silent, 125 min.
   Dir.: D.W. Griffith
   Star: Lillian Gish, Dorothy Gish

Other Voices   NTS
   USA, B/W, 100 min.
   Dir. of Hosp.: Dr. Albert M. Honig
   Mental patients at the Delaware Valley
      Mental Health Foundation

Pacific Vibrations   MAC/FREE
   USA, color
   Dir.: John Severson

The Panic in Needle Park   GENESIS
   USA, 1970, color
   Dir.: Jerry Schatzberg
   Star: Al Pacino, Kitty Winn

Paradise Now   NEWLINE
   USA, color, 95 min.
   Dir.: Sheldon Rochlin
   Star: Living Theatre

Paramount on Parade   UNIV. KIN.
   USA, 1930, B/W, new offering push, 77 min.   UNIV/16
   Star: Skeets Gallagher, Leon Errol,
      Jack Oakie, Maurice Chevalier

Paranoiac   UNIV/16
   B/W, 80 min.
   Dir.: Freddie Francis
   Star: Jeanette Scott, Oliver Reed

Paris Uprising—May 1968   NEW YORKER
   France, 1968, B/W, no subtitles, 30 min.

Pasolini, Pier Paolo   A/B
   Italy, 1970, color, English narration, 30 min.
   Dir.: Carlo Hayman-Chaffey

The Passion of Anna   UA/16
  Sweden, 1970, color, subtitled, 99 min.
  Dir.: Ingmar Bergman
  Star: Max Von Sydow, Liv Ullmann, Bibi Andersson

Paths of Glory (banned in France)   UA/16
  Gr. Br., 1957, B/W, 87 min.
  Dir.: Stanley Kubrick
  Star: Kirk Douglas, Ralph Meeker, Adolphe Menjou

Patton   FI
  USA, 1971, color, 171 min.
  Dir.: Franklin J. Schaffner
  Star: George C. Scott, Karl Malden

Paul Taylor and Company   OBERON
  USA, 1969, color, 32 min.

The Pawnbroker   A/B
  USA, 1965, B/W, 114 min.
  Dir.: Sidney Lumet
  Star: Rod Steiger

The Perils of Pauline   UNIV. KIN.
  USA, 1933, B/W, 12 chapters, 20 min. each   UNIV/16
  Dir.: Ray Taylor
  Star: Evalyn Knapp

Performance   W/B
  Gr. Br., 1970, color, 110 min.
  Dir.: Donald Cammell, Nicolas Roeg
  Star: Mick Jagger, James Fox

Persona   UA/16
  Sweden, 1967, B/W, subtitled, 81 min.
  Dir.: Ingmar Bergman
  Star: Bibi Andersson, Liv Ullmann

Peter Rabbit and the Tales of Beatrix Potter   FI
  Gr. Br., 1971, color, 98 min.
  Dir.: Reginald Mills
  Star: Britain's Royal Ballet

Le Petit Soldat   NEW YORKER
    France, 1960, B/W, subtitled, 88 min.
    Dir.: Jean-Luc Godard
    Star: Anna Karina, Michel Subor

Phantom of the Opera   UNIV. KIN.
    USA, 1943, color, sound, 93 min.   UNITED
    Dir.: Arthur Lubin
    Star: Nelson Eddy, Claude Rains

Phantom of the Opera   FI
    USA, 1925, B/W, silent, 75 min.   A/B
    FI has original music score   UNITED
    Dir.: Rupert Julian   SWANK
    Star: Lon Chaney   F. IMAGES

Pierrot Le Fou   CON
    France, 1965, color, subtitled, 110 min.
    Dir.: Jean-Luc Godard
    Star: Jean-Paul Belmondo, Anna Karina

A Plague on Your Children   TIME/LIFE
    BBC TV
    Chemical and biological warfare potential tragedy

Planet of the Apes   FI
    USA, color, 112 min.
    Dir.: Franklin Schaffner
    Star: Charlton Heston

Play Misty for Me   SWANK
    USA, 1971, color, 102 min.
    Dir.: Clint Eastwood
    Star: Clint Eastwood, Jessica Walter

The Point   A/B
    1971, color, animation, 75 min.
    Directed and Animated by Fred Wolf

Point of Order   WALTER
    USA, 1964, B/W, 97 min.   NEW YORKER
    Documentary of 1954 McCarthy hearings
    Prod.: Emile de Antonio
    Dir.: Emile de Antonio

Popcorn   BUDGET
   USA, 1969, color, 85 min.
   Star: Mick Jagger, Jimi Hendrix

Popeye Cartoons   UA/16
   Color, 25 titles, approximately 7 min. each

Portrait of Lenin (Lenin in Poland)   A/B
   USSR, 1965, B/W, English narration, 95 min.
   Dir.: Sergei Youtkevitch
   Star: Maxim Straukl

Potemkin   A/B
   USSR, 1925, B/W, subtitled, 67 min., music score   BUDGET
   Dir.: Sergei Eisenstein

Pound   UA/16
   USA, 1970, color, 92 min.
   Dir.: Robert Downey

Prague: Summer of Tanks   UNIV/16
   Czechoslovakia, 1970, subtitled, 29 min.

The President's Analyst   FI
   USA, color, 100 min.
   Star: James Coburn

The Private Life of Sherlock Holmes   UA/16
   Gr. Br., 1970, color, 125 min.
   Dir.: Billy Wilder
   Star: Robert Stephens, Colin Blakely

Privilege   UNIV. KIN.
   Gr. Br., 1967, color, 103 min.   UNITED
   Dir.: Peter Watkins   SWANK
   Star: Paul Jones, Jean Shrimpton   TWYMAN

The Producers   AVCO
   USA, color, 88 min.
   Dir.: Mel Brooks
   Star: Zero Mostel, Gene Wilder

The Professionals   COL
USA, color, 117 min.   SWANK
Dir.: Richard Brooks
Star: Burt Lancaster, Lee Marvin, Ralph Bellamy

The Projectionist   GENESIS
USA, 1971, color
Dir.: Harry Hurwitz
Star: Chuck McCann, Rodney Dangerfield

Prologue   CON
Canada, 1969, B/W, 87 min.
Dir.: Robert Spry
Star: Abbie Hoffman, Dick Gregory, J. K. Galbraith,
      William Burroughs, Allen Ginsberg, Jean Genet

Psycho   UNIV. KIN.
USA, 1960, B/W, 109 min.   SWANK
Dir.: Alfred Hitchcock   WESTCOAST
Star: Anthony Perkins, Janet Leigh, Vera Miles   UNIV/16

Punishment Park   NTS
Gr. Br., USA, 1971, color
Dir.: Peter Watkins

Purple Noon   A/B
France, 1960, color, subtitled
   or dubbed, 115 min.
Dir.: René Clement
Star: Alain Delon

Putney Swope   CIN V
Dir.: Robert Downey

The Queen   GROVE
USA, color, 68 min.
Dir.: Frank Simon
Star: Jack Doroshow, Richard Finnochio

Quiet Days in Clichy   GROVE
Denmark, B/W, English dialogue, 100 min.
Dir.: Jens Jorgen Thorson
Star: Louise White, Paul Valjean, Wayne Rodda

Rachel, Rachel　　　　　　　　　　　　　　　　A/B
　　USA, 1968, color, 101 min.　　　　　　　　　SWANK
　　Dir.: Paul Newman　　　　　　　　　　　　　CM. WMS.
　　Star: Joanne Woodward　　　　　　　　　　　WESTCOAST

Rashomon　　　　　　　　　　　　　　　　　　JANUS
　　Japan, 1950, B/W, subtitled, 83 min.
　　Dir.: Akira Kurosawa

Raven's End　　　　　　　　　　　　　　　NEW YORKER
　　Sweden, 1964, B/W, subtitled, 100 min.
　　Dir.: Bo Widerberg
　　Star: Thommy Berggren, Keve Hjelm

Rebecca　　　　　　　　　　　　　　　　　　　A/B
　　USA, 1940, B/W, 115 min.
　　Dir.: Alfred Hitchcock
　　Star: Laurence Olivier, Joan Fontaine

Rebecca of Sunnybrook Farm　　　　　　　　　FI
　　USA, B/W, 80 min.
　　Star: Shirley Temple

Rebel Without a Cause　　　　　　　　　　　　A/B
　　USA, 1955, color, 111 min.　　　　　　　　　SWANK
　　Dir.: Nicholas Ray　　　　　　　　　　　　　MSP
　　Star: James Dean, Natalie Wood,　　　　　　ARCUS
　　　　Sal Mineo, Dennis Hopper

Red China　　　　　　　　　　　　　　　　TIME/LIFE
　　BBC TV production

Red Desert　　　　　　　　　　　　　　　　　A/B
　　Italy, 1964, color, subtitled, 116 min.
　　Dir.: Michelangelo Antonioni
　　Star: Monica Vitti, Richard Harris

Reefer Madness　　　　　　　　　　　　　　NEWLINE
　　USA, 1936, B/W, 60 min.
　　Produced by U.S. Government as anti-
　　　　marijuana propaganda

The Reivers   SWANK
  USA, color, 107 min.
  Dir.: Mark Reidel
  Star: Steve McQueen

Repulsion   COL
  Gr. Br., B/W, 105 min.
  Dir.: Roman Polanski
  Star: Catherine Deneuve

Revolution   UA/16
  USA, 1968, color, 87 min.
  Dir.: Jack O'Connell
  Star: Today Malone, Herb Caen

The Revolutionary   UA/16
  USA, 1970, color, 100 min.
  Dir.: Paul Williams
  Star: Jon Voigt

Rider on the Rain   AVCO
  France, color, English dialogue, 119 min.
  Dir.: René Clement
  Star: Charles Bronson, Marlene Jobert

Right On!   NEWLINE
  USA, color, 78 min.
  Dir.: Herb Danska

The Ritual   JANUS
  Dir.: Ingmar Bergman

Road Runner Cartoons   A/B
  USA, color, 26 titles, sound, 7 min. each

Roaring Twenties   UA/16
  USA, 1939, B/W, 106 min.
  Dir.: Raoul Walsh
  Star: James Cagney, Humphrey Bogart

Rocco and His Brothers   A/B
  Italy, 1960, B/W, subtitled, 155 min.
  Dir.: Luchino Visconti
  Star: Alain Delon

Rock Around the Clock   BUDGET
                                                           ICS

Ronald Reagan Films   UA/16

Room Service   A/B
   USA, 1938, B/W, 78 min.
   Star: Marx Brothers

Rosemary's Baby   FI
   USA, color, 136 min.
   Dir.: Roman Polanski
   Star: Mia Farrow, John Cassavetes

Rush to Judgment   A/D
   USA, 1967, B/W, 90 min.
   Dir.: Emile de Antonio

Sad Song of Yellow Skin   FI
   Color, 58 min., Vietnam documentary
   Dir.: Michael Rubbo
   National Film Board, Canada

Salesman   NTS
   USA, 1966, B/W, 90 min.
   Dir.: Maysles Brothers

Sallah   MAKOR
   Israel, B/W, subtitled, 105 min.

Salt of the Earth   A/D
   1954, B/W, 94 min.   A/B
   Dir.: Herbert Biberman

Samurai   A/B
   Japan, 1954, color, subtitled, 92 min.
   Dir.: Hiroshi Inagaki
   Star: Toshiro Mifune

The Sand Pebbles   FI
   USA, color, 152 min.
   Dir.: Robert Wise
   Star: Steve McQueen, Richard Attenborough,
      Candice Bergen

Santanis The Devil's Mass   BUDGET
USA, 1972, color, 70 min.
Dir.: Ray Laurent

Mr. Sardonicus   MSP
Star: Oscar Homolka

Sayarim   MAKOR
Israel, B/W, subtitled, 96 min.
Star: Assaf Dayan

Scrooge   SWANK
Gr. Br., color, 111 min.
Dir.: Ronald Neame
Star: Albert Finney, Alec Guinness

The Sea Around Us   FI
Based on novel by Rachel Carson
USA, color, 61 min.

The Sea Wolf   UA/16
USA, 1941, B/W, 95 min.   A/B
Based on novel by Jack London
Dir.: Michael Curitz
Star: Edward G. Robinson, Ida Lupino, Barry Fitzgerald

Seadreams   MAC/FREE
USA, color

Seance on a Wet Afternoon   A/B
Gr. Br., 1964, B/W, 115 min.
Dir.: Bryan Forbes
Star: Richard Attenborough, Kim Stanley

Secret Ceremony   UNIV. KIN.
Gr. Br., 1969, color, 109 min.   UNITED
Dir.: Joseph Losey   SWANK
Star: Elizabeth Taylor, Mia Farrow, Robert Mitchum   UNIV/16

Seduced and Abandoned   WALTER
Italy, 1964, B/W, subtitled, 90 min.
Dir.: Pietro Germi
Star: Paola Biggio, Stefania Sandrelli

The Selling of the Pentagon   A/D
   USA, 1971, B/W, 54 min.
   CBS News documentary

The Servant   A/B
   Gr. Br., 1963, B/W, 115 min.
   Dir.: Joseph Losey
   Star: Dirk Bogarde, Sarah Miles

Seven Samurai (Magnificent Seven)   A/B
   Japan, 1954, B/W, subtitled, 141 min.
   Dir.: Akira Kurosawa
   Star: Toshiro Mifune

The Seventh Seal   JANUS
   Sweden, 1956, B/W, subtitled, 96 min.
   Dir.: Ingmar Bergman

Shadows of Forgotten Ancestors   JANUS
(Wild Horses of Fire)
   Russia, color, 80 min.
   Dir.: Serge Parajanov

Shaft   FI
   USA, 1971, color, 98 min.
   Dir.: Gordon Parks
   Star: Richard Roundtree, Moses Gunn

Shame   UA/16
   Sweden, 1969, B/W, subtitled, 102 min.
   Dir.: Ingmar Bergman
   Star: Liv Ullmann, Max Von Sydow

Shanghai Express   UNIV. KIN.
   USA, 1932, B/W, 84 min.   UNITED
   Dir.: Josef Von Sternberg   UNIV/16
   Star: Marlene Dietrich, Anna May Wong

She Done Him Wrong   UNIV. KIN.
   USA, 1933, B/W, 68 min.   UNITED
   Dir.: Lowell Sherman   UNIV/16
   Star: Mae West, Cary Grant   WESTCOAST

Sherlock Holmes   UNITED
  Twelve features
  Star: Basil Rathbone, Nigel Bruce

Ship of Fools   A/B
  USA, 1965, B/W, 149 min.
  Dir.: Stanley Kramer
  Star: Simone Signoret, Oskar Werner

Shoot the Piano Player   JANUS
  France, 1960, B/W, subtitled, 84 min.
  Dir.: François Truffaut

The Shop on Main Street   A/B
  Czechoslovakia, 1965, B/W, subtitled, 128 min.
  Dir.: Jan Kadar
  Star: Josepf Kroner, Ida Kaminska

The Sicilian Clan   FI
  France, color, 121 min.
  Dir.: Henri Verneuil
  Star: Alain Delon

Sierra Club Film Library   CCM
  Redwoods-Saved?
  Glen Canyon
  The Grand Canyon
  1/40th of a Federal Forest
  Two Yosemites
  Nature Next Door
  An Island In Time   ·
  Wilderness Alps of Stehekin
  No Room for Wilderness?
  The Redwoods
  Wasted Woods
  Miner's Ridge
  Wilderness River Trail
  Mineral King

The Silence   JANUS
  Sweden, 1963, B/W, subtitled, 95 min.
  Dir.: Ingmar Bergman

The Silent World   CON
France, 1956, color, English dialogue, 86 min.   A/B
Dir.: Jacques-Yves Cousteau, Louis Malle

Simon of the Desert   A/B
Mexico, 1965, B/W, subtitled, 43 min.
Dir.: Luis Buñuel
Star: Silvia Pinal, Claudio Brook

Sixty Hours to Suez   MAKOR
Israel, B/W, subtitled, 100 min.
Israel/Arab six-day war filmed by Israeli cameramen

Ski on the Wild Side   A/B
USA, 1967, color, 104 min.
Dir., Prod. and Narr.: Warren Miller

The Sky Above, the Mud Below   A/B
France, 1961, color, English dialogue, 90 min.
Dir.: Pierre-Dominque Gaisseau

The Sky Pirate   NEWLINE
USA, color, 85 min.
Dir.: Andrew Meyer
Star: Michael McClanathan, Joy Bang

Slaughterhouse Five   SWANK
USA, 1972, color, 104 min.
Dir.: George Roy Hill
Star: Michael Saks, Sharon Gans

The Sleeping Car Murder   A/B
Dir.: Costa Gravas
Star: Yves Montand, Simone Signoret

Snow Country   F. IMAGES
Japan, 1957, subtitled, 120 min.
Dir.: Shiro Toyoda
Star: Ryo Ikebe, Keiko Kishi, Kaoru Yachigusa
From novel by Y. Kawabata

Socrates   NEW YORKER
France–Italy–Spain, 1970, color, subtitled, 120 min.
Dir.: Roberto Rossellini

Sodom and Gomorrah   FI
   USA, color, 154 min.
   Star: Stewart Granger, Anouk Aimee

The Soft Skin   COL
   France, B/W, subtitled or dubbed, 119 min.
   Dir.: François Truffaut
   Star: Jean Desailly, François Dorleac

Soldier Blue   AVCO
   USA, 1969, color, 112 min.
   Dir.: Ralph Nelson
   Star: Candice Bergen, Peter Strauss, Donald Pleasance

Sometimes a Great Notion   SWANK
   USA, 1971, color, 110 min.
   Star: Paul Newman, Henry Fonda

Son of the Sheik   A/B
   USA, 1926, B/W, silent, music score, 72 min.   CON
   Dir.: George Fitzmaurice   F. IMAGES
   Star: Rudolph Valentino

Sons and Daughters   A/D
   USA, 1965, B/W, 90 min.
   Prod.: Jerry Stoll

The Sorrow and the Pity   CIN V

Soul to Soul   SWANK
   USA, 1971, 96 min.
   Dir.: Denis Sanders
   Star: Wilson Pickett, Ike and Tina Turner, Santana

The Spanish Earth   A/D
   USA, 1937, B/W, 54 min.   A/B
   Written and narrated by Ernest Hemingway

Spies   JANUS
   Germany, 1928, B/W, 90 min.
   Dir.: Fritz Lang

Spirits of the Dead   WESTCOAST
   Italy, 1969, color, subtitled, 95 min.
   Co-Dir.: Federico Fellini
   Star: Jane Fonda, Alain Delon, Terence Stamp

Stagolee: Bobby Seale in Prison   A/D
   USA, 1970, B/W, 60 min.
   KQED, San Francisco, documentary

Stalag 17   FI
   USA, B/W, 120 min.
   Dir.: Billy Wilder
   Star: William Holden, Otto Preminger

The Stalking Moon   FI
   USA, color, 105 min.
   Dir.: Robert Mulligan
   Star: Gregory Peck, Eva Marie Saint

Stolen Kisses   UA/16
   France, 1969, color, subtitled, 90 min.
   Dir.: François Truffaut
   Star: Jean-Pierre Léaude, Delphine Seyrig

La Strada   A/B
   Italy, B/W, subtitled
   Dir.: Federico Fellini
   Star: Giulietta Masina, Anthony Quinn

Straw Dogs   FI
   Gr. Br., 1971, color, 118 min.
   Dir.: Sam Peckinpath
   Star: Dustin Hoffman, Susan George

Summer of '42   W/B
   USA, 1971
   Dir.: Robert Mulligan
   Star: Jennifer O'Neill

Sundays and Cybelle   COL
   France, B/W, subtitled, 110 min.
   Dir.: Serge Bourguignon
   Star: Hardy Kruger, Patricia Gozzi

Sweet Sweetback's Baadasssss Song   W/B
    USA, 1970, color
    Dir.: Melvin Van Peebles

Sweet Toronto   L/P
    USA, 1969, color, feature
    Dir.: Leacock/Pennebaker
    Rock concert

Sympathy for the Devil   NEWLINE
    Gr. Br., color, 110 min.
    Dir.: Jean-Luc Godard
    Star: The Rolling Stones

THX-1138   W/B
    USA, 1970
    Dir.: George Lucas
    Star: Robert Duvall, Maggie McOmie

Taking Off   SWANK
    USA, 1970, color, 92 min.
    Dir.: Milos Forman
    Star: Buck Henry, Lynn Carlin

Tarzan the Ape Man   FI
    1932, Van Dyke

Tarzan and His Mate
    1934, Conway/Gibbons

Tarzan Escapes
    1936, McKay/Farrow/Thorpe

Tell Them Willie Boy Is Here   SWANK
    USA, 1970, color, 98 min.   WESTCOAST
    Dir.: Abraham Polonsky
    Star: Robert Redford, Katherine Ross

The Tenth Victim   A/B
    Italy, 1965, color, subtitled, 92 min.
    Dir.: Elio Petri
    Star: Marcello Mastroianni, Ursula Andress

Teorema   WALTER
   Italy, 1969, color, subtitled, 93 min.
   Dir.: Pier Paolo Pasolini
   Star: Laura Betti, Massimo Girotti, Terence Stamp

They Shoot Horses, Don't They?   FI
   USA, color, 129 min.
   Dir.: Sydney Pollack
   Star: Jane Fonda, Susannah York, Gig Young

The Thief of Bagdad   A/B
   USA, 1924, B/W, silent, 133 min.   SWANK
   Dir.: Raoul Walsh
   Star: Douglas Fairbanks

A Thousand Clowns   UA/16
   USA, 1966, B/W, 118 min.
   Dir.: Fred Coe
   Star: Jason Robards, Barbara Harris

The 1,000 Eyes of Dr. Mabuse   A/B
   Germany, 1960, dubbed, English dialogue, 97 min.
   Dir.: Fritz Lang
   Star: Peter Van Eyck

This Sporting Life   WALTER
   Gr. Br., 1963, B/W, 126 min.
   Dir.: Lindsay Anderson
   Star: Richard Harris, Rachel Roberts

Throne of Blood   A/B
   Japan, 1957, B/W, subtitled, 105 min.
   Dir.: Akira Kurosawa
   Star: Toshiro Mifune

Through a Glass Darkly   JANUS
   Sweden, B/W, subtitled
   Dir.: Ingmar Bergman

The Time Machine   FI
   Adapted from H.G. Wells' novel
   USA, color, 103 min.
   Dir.: George Paul
   Star: Rod Taylor, Yvette Mimieux

Titicut Follies   GROVE
USA, B/W, 85 min.
Dir.: Frederick Wiseman
Star: inmates of state prison hospital in
    Bridgewater, Massachusetts

Tom Jones   UA/16
Gr. Br., 1963, color, 127 min.
Dir.: Tony Richardson
Star: Albert Finney, Susannah York

Tora, Tora, Tora   FI
USA, 1970, color, 143 min.
Dir.: Richard Fleischer, Toshido Masuda
Star: Martin Balsam, Joseph Cotten, E. G. Marshall

Torment   JANUS
Sweden, 1944, B/W, subtitled, 90 min.
Dir.: A. Sjoberg

The Touch   FI
USA/Sweden, 1971, color, 112 min.
Dir.: Ingmar Bergman
Star: Elliott Gould, Bibi Andersson

Transatlantic Tunnel   JANUS
Gr. Br., 1935, B/W, 94 min.

Trash   CIN V
Dir.: Paul Morrisey
Star: Joe Dallesandro

The Treasure of the Sierra Madre   A/B
USA, 1948, B/W, 126 min.   CON
Dir.: John Huston   FI
Star: Humphrey Bogart   UA/16
                                                     CM. WMS.

Treasure Island   FI
USA, 1934, B/W, 95 min.
Dir.: Victor Fleming
Star: Wallace Beery, Jackie Cooper, Lionel Barrymore

Treasure Island   BUDGET
  USA, color, 60 min.
  Animated Version

The Trial
  France, 1962, B/W, English dialogue, 118 min.
  Dir., Prod. and Written by Orson Welles
  Star: Anthony Perkins, Orson Welles, Jeanne Moreau
  Based on novel by Franz Kafka

Trial of Joan of Arc   CON
  France, 1962, B/W, subtitled, 65 min.
  Dir.: Robert Bresson
  Star: Florence Carrez, Jean-Claude Fourneau

Tricia's Wedding   GROVE
  USA, 1970, color, 35 min.
  Star: The Cockettes

The Trip   BUDGET
  USA, 1967, color, 85 min.   A/B
  Screenplay: Jack Nicholson   WESTCOAST
  Dir.: Roger Corman
  Star: Peter Fonda, Dennis Hopper

Tristana   A/B
  Spain, 1970, color, subtitled, 95 min.
  Dir.: Luis Buñuel
  Star: Catherine Deneuve, Fernando Rey

Triumph of the Will   CON
  Documentary of a propaganda rally during the   A/B
    Third Reich. Film commissioned by Adolf Hitler.
  Germany, 1934–36, subtitled, 120 min.
  Dir.: Leni Riefenstahl

The Trojan Women   SWANK
  1971, color, 105 min.
  Dir.: Michael Cacoyannis
  Star: Katherine Hepburn, Vanessa Redgrave, Irene Papas

Twisted Cross   MSP
  Story of Adolf Hitler recreated from German news film

Two Daughters   JANUS
    India, 1961, subtitled, 114 min.
    Dir.: Satyajit Ray

Two Lane Blacktop   SWANK
    USA, 1970, color, 102 min.
    Dir.: Monte Hellman
    Star: James Taylor

Two Mules for Sister Sara   UNIV/16
    USA, 1970, color, 105 min.
    Dir.: Don Siegal
    Star: Clint Eastwood, Shirley MacLaine

Two or Three Things I Know About Her   NEW YORKER
    France, 1966, color, subtitled, 85 min.
    Dir.: Jean-Luc Godard
    Star: Marina Vlady

2001: A Space Odyssey   FI
    Gr. Br., color, 160 min.
    Dir.: Stanley Kubrick
    Star: Keir Dullea

Two Women   A/B
    Italy, 1961, B/W, dubbed or
        subtitled, 105 min.
    Dir.: Vittorio De Sica
    Star: Sophia Loren, Jean-Paul Belmondo

UPA Cartoons   A/B
    Mister Magoo
    Gerald McBoing Boing
    USA, color, sound, 8 min. each, 28 titles

Ulysses   WALTER
    Gr. Br., 1967, B/W, 132 min.
    Adapted from James Joyce's novel
    Dir.: Joseph Strick
    Star: Barbara Jefford, Anna Manahan, Milo O'Shea

The Umbrellas of Cherbourg   A/B
    France, 1964, color, subtitled, 90 min.
    Dir.: Jacques Demy
    Star: Catherine Deneuve

Vampyr   A/B
  Germany, 1931, B/W, subtitled, 66 min.
  Dir.: Carl Dreyer
  Star: Julian West, Henrietta Gerard

Vanishing Prairie   MSP
  Walt Disney Production   FI
  USA, color, 71 min.

Le Viol   UNITED
  France, color, subtitled, 78 min.
  Dir.: Jacques Doniol-Valcroze
  Star: Bibi Andersson

The Virgin President   NEWLINE
  B/W, 90 min.
  Dir.: Graeme Fergusen
  Star: Svern Darden

Virgin Spring   JANUS
  Sweden, 1959, B/W, subtitled, 88 min.
  Dir.: Ingmar Bergman

Viridiana   A/B
  Spain, 1961, B/W, subtitled, 90 min.
  Dir.: Luis Buñuel
  Star: Silvia Pinal, Fernando Rey

Viva La Muerte   NEWLINE
  France, 1970, B/W, subtitled
  Dir.: Fornando Arrabal
  Star: Mahdi Chabuch

Viva Zapata   FI
  B/W, 113 min.
  Dir.: Elia Kazan
  Star: Marlon Brando, Anthony Quinn

WR-Mysteries of the Organism   CIN V

W.U.S.A.   FI
  USA, 1971, color, 115 min.
  Dir.: Stuart Rosenberg
  Star: Paul Newman, Joanne Woodward

The Wages of Fear   A/B
    France, 1953, B/W, subtitled, 138 min.

Wait Until Dark   A/B
    USA, 1967, color, 107 min.   SWANK
    Dir.: Terence Young   MSP
    Star: Audrey Hepburn, Alan Arkin   CM. WMS.
                                                        WESTCOAST
                                                        "THE" F.C.
                                                        BUDGET

Waiting for Godot   GROVE
    USA, B/W, 102 min.
    Dir.: Alan Schneider
    Star: Zero Mostel, Burgess Meredith

Walkabout   FI
    Australia, 1970, color, 95 min.
    Dir.: Nicolas Roeg
    Star: Jenny Agutter, Lucien John

Wall in Jerusalem   EYR
    1969, B/W, 91 min.
    Dir.: Frederic Rossif

War and Peace   WALTER
    Russia, 1968, color, dubbed   (35MM ONLY)
    Part I, 195 min.
    Part II, 178 min.
    Prod.: Mosfilm
    Dir.: Sergei Bondarchuk
    Star: Sergei Bondarchuk, Vasily Lanovoi, Irini Skobtseva

The War Game   CON
    Gr. Br., 1965, B/W, 47 min.
    Written and Dir.: Peter Watkins

Warrendale   GROVE
    Canada, 1967, B/W, 105 min.
    Dir.: Allan King
    Emotionally disturbed children at their
       treatment center in Toronto, Canada

Warsaw Ghetto　　　　　　　　　　　　　　　　　　　TIME/LIFE
　　Germany, 1940, B/W, 51 min.

Weekend　　　　　　　　　　　　　　　　　　　　　　GROVE
　　France, color, subtitled, 105 min.
　　Dir.: Jean-Luc Godard

Werewolf of London　　　　　　　　　　　　　　　　　UNITED
　　B/W, 74 min.
　　Star: Henry Hull, Warner Oland

When Comedy Was King　　　　　　　　　　　　　　　CON
　　USA, 1960, B/W, 90 min.　　　　　　　　　　　　　　A/B
　　Prod.: Robert Yonngston　　　　　　　　　　　　　　MSP
　　Sequences featuring Charlie Chaplin, Buster Keaton,
　　　　Laurel and Hardy and many others. Harry Langdon,
　　　　Fatty Arbuckle, Gloria Swanson.
　　Includes time from 1914–28.

Where's Poppa?　　　　　　　　　　　　　　　　　　UA/16
　　USA, 1970, color, 87 min.
　　Dir.: Carl Reiner
　　Star: George Segal, Ruth Gordon

The White Shiek　　　　　　　　　　　　　　　　　　CON
　　Italy, 1952, B/W, subtitled, 86 min.
　　Dir.: Federico Fellini
　　Star: Alberto Sordi, Guilietta Massina

Wild Rovers　　　　　　　　　　　　　　　　　　　　FI
　　USA, 1971, color, 110 min.
　　Dir.: Blake Edwards
　　Star: Ryan O'Neal, William Holden

Winning　　　　　　　　　　　　　　　　　　　　　UNIV/16
　　1969, color, 123 min.
　　Dir.: James Goldstone
　　Star: Paul Newman, Joanne Woodward

Who Is Harry Kellerman and Why Is He　　　　　　　SWANK
Saying Those Terrible Things About Me?
　　USA, 1970, color, 139 min.
　　Dir.: Ulu Grosbard
　　Star: Dustin Hoffman

Who's Afraid of Virginia Woolf?   w/b
   USA, 1966, B/W, 129 min.
   Dir.: Mike Nichols
   Star: Elizabeth Taylor, Richard Burton,
       Sandy Dennis, George Segal

Why Not   NEWLINE
   USA, color, 116 min.
   Dir.: Arakawa

The Wild Bunch   w/b
   USA, 1970, color, 135 min.
   Dir.: Sam Peckinpah
   Star: William Holden, Ernest Borgnine, Warren Oates

The Wild Child   ua/16
   France, 1970, B/W, subtitled, 85 min.
   Dir.: François Truffaut
   Star: François Truffaut, Jean-Pierre Cargol

Wild in the Streets   a/b
   USA, 1968, color, 96 min.   UPA
   Dir.: Barry Shear   WESTCOAST
   Star: Christopher Jones, Richard Pryor   BUDGET

The Wild One   MSP
   USA, 1953, B/W, 79 min.
   Dir.: Stanley Kramer
   Star: Marlon Brando, Lee Marvin

Wild Strawberries   JANUS
   Sweden, 1957, B/W, subtitled, 90 min.
   Dir.: Ingmar Bergman

Willard   SWANK
   USA, 1971, color, 95 min.
   Dir.: Daniel Mann
   Star: Ernest Borgnine

Witchcraft Thru the Ages   JANUS
(Haxan)
   Sweden, 1922, B/W, 90 min.
   Dir.: Benjamin Christensen

The Wizard of Oz   FI
USA, color, 101 min.
Dir.: Victor Fleming
Star: Judy Garland, Ray Bolger

Woman in the Dunes   CON
Japan, 1964, B/W, subtitled, 123 min.
Dir.: Hiroshi Teshigahara
Star: Eiji Okada, Kyoko Kishida

Women In Love   UA/16
From novel by D.H. Lawrence
Gr. Br., 1970, color, 129 min.
Dir.: Ken Russell
Star: Alan Bates, Oliver Reed, Glenda Jackson

Women in Revolt   NEWLINE
USA, 1971, color, feature
Dir.: Andy Warhol
Star: Candy Darling, Holly Woodlawn, Jackie Curtis

Woodstock   W/B
USA, 1970, color, 183 min.
Dir.: Michael Wadleigh
Star: Jimi Hendrix; Crosby, Stills, Nash and Young;
    plus 400,000 other beautiful people

The World of Apu   A/B
India, 1959, B/W, English dialogue, 103 min.
Dir.: Satyajit Ray
Music: Ravi Shankar

The World of Henry Orient   UA/16
USA, 1964, color, 106 min.
Dir.: George Roy Hill
Star: Peter Sellers, Paula Prentiss

World Without Sun   CON
France, 1964, color, English narration, 93 min.
Dir.: Jacques-Yves Cousteau
Academy Award-winning documentary

The Year of the Communes   ASSOC.
   USA, 1969, color, 52 min.
   Dir.: Chris Munger

Years of Lightning, Day of Drums   AVCO
   Dir.: Bruce Herschensohn
   Commentary: Gregory Peck
   The two-years, ten-month Presidency of JFK

Yojimbo   JANUS
   Japan, 1961, B/W, subtitled, 110 min.   A/B
   Dir.: Akira Kurosawa
   Star: Toshiro Mifune

Young Aphrodites   JANUS
   Greece, 1964, B/W, subtitled, 87 min.
   Dir.: Nikos Koundouros

Young Toerless   CON
   Germany, 1966, B/W, subtitled, 87 min.
   Dir.: Volker Schondorf
   Star: Matthieu Carriere, Barbara Steele

You're a Big Boy Now   W/B
   USA, 1965, color, 97 min.
   Dir.: Francis Ford Coppola
   Star: Rip Torn, Peter Kastner

Z   CIN V
   Dir.: Costa Gavras
   Star: Yves Montand

Zabriskie Point   FI
   USA, color, 112 min.
   Dir.: Michelangelo Antonioni
   Star: Mark Frechette, Daria Halprin

Zachariah   FI
   USA, 1971, color, 92 min.
   Dir.: George Englund
   Star: Don Johnson, John Rubenstein

Zazie   NEW YORKER
    France, 1960, color, 90 min.   (35MM ONLY)
    Dir.: Louis Malle

Zazie Dans Le Métro   CON
(Zazie and the Subway)
    France, 1960, color, subtitled, 85 min.
    Dir.: Louis Malle
    Star: Catherine Demongeot, Philippe Noiret

Zoos of the World   TIME/LIFE
    Series of eight films
    1 & 2—San Diego
        3—Antwerp
        4—Tucson
        5—West Berlin
        6—London
        7—Basel
        8—Frankfurt

Zorba the Greek
    USA, B/W, 142 min.
    Star: Anthony Quinn, Alan Bates,
          Irene Papas, Lila Kedrova

8

Distributors

A.C.I. Films, Inc. 35 West 45th Street New York, N.Y. 10036	American and foreign shorts
Altura Films International 225 East 46th Street New York, N.Y. 10017	35mm non-theatrical classics
American Documentary Films 336 W. 84th Street New York, N.Y. 10024 379 Bay Street San Francisco, Calif. 94133	Socio/political documentaries; Cuban and Vietnamese films
American Educational Films 9304 Santa Monica Boulevard Beverly Hills, Calif. 90210	Educational films
American Entertainment 52 West 8th Street New York, N.Y. 10011	*Hendrix at Berkeley,* 16mm and 35mm
Amerpol Enterprises 11601 Joseph Campau Avenue Detroit, Mich. 48212	Polish features

Argus Films
   1225 Broadway
   New York, N.Y.   10001

English language features and shorts

Artkino Pictures
   165 W. 46th Street   Room 910
   New York, N.Y.   10036

35mm Soviet films

Association/Sterling Films
   600 Madison Avenue
   New York, N.Y.   10022

Free loan educational documentaries

Audio/Brandon Film Center
   34 Macquesten Parkway South
   Mount Vernon, N.Y.   10550
   406 Clement Street
   San Francisco, Calif.   94118
   1619 North Cherokee
   Los Angeles, Calif.   90028
   8615 Directors Row
   Dallas, Texas, 75247
   512 Burlington Avenue
   La Grange, Ill.   60525

American and foreign-language
   features and shorts; also
   experimental features and shorts,
   American and foreign

AVCO Embassy Pictures Corp.
   1301 Avenue of the Americas
   New York, N.Y.   10010

American features

Azteca Films
   132 W. 43rd Street
   New York, N.Y.   10036

Spanish-language features; 35mm
   available

Bailey Film Associates
   11559 Santa Monica Boulevard
   Los Angeles, Calif.   90025

Educational documentaries

Billy Budd Films
   235 East 57th Street   Room 8D
   New York, N.Y.   10022

Educational documentaries

Black Star Productions
   19230 James Couzens
   Detroit, Michigan   48235

"Al Fateh Palestinians"

Budget Films
   4590 Santa Monica Boulevard
   Los Angeles, Calif.   90029

English-language features, silents,
   serials, some foreign films, shorts

CBS/Holt Group
383 Madison Avenue
New York, N.Y.   10017

CBS-TV documentaries

CCM Films
866 Third Avenue
New York, N.Y.   10022

Educational documentaries,
environmental

University of California
Extension Medea Center
Berkeley, Calif.   94720

Educational documentaries

Canyon Cinema Cooperative
Room 220,
Industrial Center Building
Sausalito, Calif.   94965

Also 8mm, experimental
"underground" shorts, some features

Carousel Films, Inc.
1501 Broadway
New York, N.Y.   10036

Educational documentaries

Center Cinema Coop.
c/o Columbia College
540 North Lake Shore Drive
Chicago, Ill.   60611

Experimental "underground" films

Centron Educational Films
1621 W. 9th Street
Lawrence, Kansas   66044

Educational documentaries

Charard Motion Pictures
2110 East 24th Street
Brooklyn, N.Y.   11229

American features and shorts

Charlou Productions
165 W. 46th Street
New York, N.Y.   10036

English-language features

Children's Cultural Foundation
325 East 57th Street
New York, N.Y.   10022

Films by New York teenagers

Churchill Films
662 North Robertson Boulevard
Los Angeles, Calif.   90069

Films by teenagers

Cinema V
595 Madison Avenue
New York, N.Y.   10022

American and foreign features,
16mm and 35mm

9255 Sunset Boulevard
Suite 402
Los Angeles, Calif.   90069

Cinema Service Corp.
106 West End Avenue
New York, N.Y.   10023

Yiddish film classics

Cinema Ventures
133 W. 14th Street
New York, N.Y.   10011

Bresson/Mizoguchi films

Columbia Cinematheque
711 Fifth Avenue
New York, N.Y.   10022

American and foreign-language
features

Columbia University Press
Center for Mass Communications
440 W. 110th Street
New York, N.Y.   10025

Educational documentaries

Contemporary Films/McGraw Hill
330 West 42nd Street
New York, N.Y.   10036
1714 Stockton Street
San Francisco, Calif.   94132
828 Custer Avenue
Evanston, Ill.   60202
Princeton Road
Hightstown, N.J.   08520

American and foreign-language
features and shorts.
Pathe Contemporary,
35mm only,
330 W. 42nd Street,
New York, N.Y.   10036

Coronet Films
65 East South Water Street
Chicago, Ill.   60601

Educational

Creative Film Society
14558 Valerio Street
Van Nuys, Calif.   91405

Experimental "underground," some
features

E.Y.R. Campus Programs
78 East 56th Street
New York, N.Y.   10022

Foreign and American features,
featurettes and shorts

**Encyclopedia Britannica
Educational Corp.**
425 North Michigan Avenue
Chicago, Ill.   60611

Educational documentaries

F.I. Cultural Films
  1564 Broadway
  New York, N.Y.   10036
  203 N. Wabash Avenue
  Chicago, Ill.   60601

American and foreign-language features

"The" Film Center
  915 12th Street, N.W.
  Washington, D.C.   20005

English-language features and shorts

Film Classic Exchange
  1926 South Vermont Avenue
  Los Angeles, Calif.   90007

American and foreign-language silent and sound film classics; vintage newsreels; 35mm also

Film Images/Radim Films Inc.
  1034 Lake Street
  Oak Park, Ill.   60301
  17 W. 60th Street
  New York, N.Y.   10023

American and foreign-language features, four shorts; 35mm also

Film-Makers Cooperative
  175 Lexington Avenue
  New York, N.Y.   10016

Experimental "underground" features and shorts

Films, Inc.
  277 Pharr Road, N.E.
  Atlanta, Georgia   30305
  161 Massachusetts Avenue
  Boston, Mass.   02115
  1414 Dragon Street
  Dallas, Texas   75207
  98 W. Jackson Street   Suite 1
  Hayward, Calif.   94544
  5625 Hollywood Boulevard
  Long Island City, N.Y.   11101
  44 East South Temple
  Salt Lake City, Utah   84110
  4420 Oakton Street
  Skokie, Ill.   60076
  1144 Wilmette Avenue
  Wilmette, Ill.   60091

Mainly American features; also classics

Films for Social Change
  5122 Waterman Boulevard
  St. Louis, Mo.   63108

Socio-political documentaries

Gendon Films
P.O. Box 608
Station B
Montreal 110
Quebec, Canada

Foreign-language features

Genesis Films
1040 North Las Palmas Avenue
Los Angeles, Calif.   90038

American and foreign-language
features, experimental shorts

Baylis Glascock Films
1017 N. La Cienega Boulevard
Suite 305
Los Angeles, Calif.   90069

Multi-screen experimental films

William Greaves Productions
254 W. 54th Street
New York, N.Y.   10019

In the company of men

Grove Press, Inc.
214 Mercer Street
New York, N.Y.   10012

American and foreign-language
features and shorts; experimental
"underground" features and shorts

Hurlock Cine-World
13 Arcadia Road
Old Greenwich, Conn.   06870

Cinema novo Brazil
American and foreign-language
features

Ideal Pictures
See Films, Inc.

Impact Films
144 Bleecker Street
New York, N.Y.   10012

American and foreign features by
independent film-makers

Institutional Cinema Service
915 Broadway
New York, N.Y.   10010
67 East Madison
Chicago, Ill.   60603

American and foreign-language
features and shorts

Intermedia Artists Corp.
1974 Massachusetts Avenue
Cambridge, Mass.   02140

Experimental films

International Film Bureau
332 South Michigan Avenue
Chicago, Ill.   60604

International Film Foundation, Inc.
   475 Fifth Avenue   Room 916
   New York, N.Y.   10017

International Tournee of Animation   Animated shorts
   P.O. Box 31348
   San Francisco, Calif.   94131

Also contact: United States National Student Association
                2115 S Street   S.W.
                Washington, D.C.   20008

Ivy Films, Inc./16mm   American and foreign-language
   120 East 56th Street   features, serials; classic comedy
   New York, N.Y.   10022

Janus Films   Predominantly foreign-language
   745 Fifth Avenue   features, classics
   New York, N.Y.   10022

Leacock-Pennebaker, Inc.   American and foreign independent
   56 W. 45th Street   features and shorts,
   New York, N.Y.   10036   16mm and 35mm

Learning Corp. of America   Educational documentaries
   711 Fifth Avenue
   New York, N.Y.   10022

MacGillivray-Freeman Films   Surfing films,
   Box 205   16mm and 35mm
   South Laguna, Calif. 92677

Makor Films   Israeli films, features and featurettes
   One Continental Avenue
   Forest Hills, N.Y.   11375

Mass Media Associates, Inc.   Educational
   2116 No. Charles Street
   Baltimore, Md.   21218
   1720 Chouteau Avenue
   St. Louis, Mo. 63103

Modern Sound Pictures   American features, silents and shorts
   1410 Howard Street
   Omaha, Neb.   68102

Modern Talking Picture Service
1212 Avenue of the Americas
New York, N.Y.   10036

Educational documentaries

Monument Film Corp.
144 Bleecker Street
New York, N.Y.   10012

Independent features

Museum of Modern Art
11 West 53rd Street
New York, N.Y.   10019

American and foreign films from
1895 to present; features, shorts,
newsreels, documentaries,
experimental shorts

Richard Myers
1224 North Mantua Street
Kent, Ohio   44240

Independent film-maker—his own
films

NBC Educational Enterprises
30 Rockerfeller Plaza
New York, N.Y.   10020

NBC-TV documentaries

Ronald Nameth Films
1003 West Clark Street
Urbana, Ill.   61801

Films on artists

National Talent Service
115 East 62nd Street
New York, N.Y.   10021

Films—classics and independent
contemporary features, shorts;
lecture division includes key
prominent film-makers with their
films; video-tape rentals (groove
tube)

New Day Films
267 W. 25th Street
New York, N.Y. 10001

Films about women

New Yorker Films
2409 Broadway
New York, N.Y.   10024

Foreign-language features and classics;
35mm also

Newline Cinema
121 University Place
New York, N.Y.   10003

Independent new-wave features and
shorts; 35mm also

Newsreel
322 Seventh Avenue
New York, N.Y.   10001
595 Massachusetts Avenue
Cambridge, Mass.   02139

Political documentaries; Cuban and
Vietnamese films; new-left newsreel
shorts and features

1406 Tennessee Street
Lawrence, Kansas   66044

P.O. Box 7585
Oakland Station
Pittsburgh, Pa.   15213

1232 Market Street   Room 104
San Francisco, Calif.   94102

Newenhouse-Novo   Educational films, documentaries
1825 Willow Road
Northfield, Ill.   60093

Vaughn Obern   "*Hey, Mama*"
922-D 14th Street
Santa Monica, Calif.   90403

Oberon Communications   Dance films
236 West 101st Street
New York, N.Y.   10025

Paradigm Film Distributors
6305 Yucca Street
Los Angeles, Calif.   90028

Pigeon Productions   Documentaries
161 Mariner Street
Buffalo, N.Y.   14201

Pictura Films   Unusual shorts
43 W. 16th Street
New York, N.Y.   10011

Pyramid Film Producers   Documentary, independent and
P.O. Box 1048   shorts; some features
Santa Monica, Calif.   90406

Neil Reichline   Documentary on David Harris
1651 Veteran Avenue #6
Los Angeles, Calif.   90024

ROA's Films   American and foreign features, shorts
1696 North Astor Street
Milwaukee, Wis.   53202

Rogosin Films   Experimental, documentary, American
144 Bleecker Street   and foreign features and shorts
New York, N.Y.   10012

Roninfilm, Inc.
226 West 47th Street
New York, N.Y. 10036

American and foreign classics, 16mm and 35mm

Samuel Goldwyn/16
1041 North Formosa Avenue
Los Angeles, Calif.   90046

American features

Al Sherman
890 West End Avenue
New York, N.Y.   10025

Shorts, American, 35mm foreign films

Sherpix Films
1501 Broadway
New York, N.Y.   10036

35mm, sexploitation—some Warhol in 16mm

Sigma III Corp.
444 Madison Avenue
New York, N.Y.   10022

35mm only, foreign films

Bill Snyder
P.O. Box 2784
Fargo, North Dakota   58102

Ecology films ("Cry of the Marsh")

Barry Spinello
5166 Miles Avenue
Oakland, Calif.   94618

Abstract experimental films

Swank Motion Pictures
2151 Marion Place
Baldwin, Long Island,
N.Y.   11510
201 South Jefferson Avenue
St. Louis, Mo.   63166
2325 San Jacinto
Houston, Texas   77002
7073 Vineland Avenue
North Hollywood, Calif.   91605

American and foreign-language features, shorts, underground programs, cartoons; 16mm and 35mm

Theodore Holcomb
11 E. 90th Street
New York, N.Y.   10028

"Russia"

Third World Cinema Group
2121 Browning
Berkeley, Calif.   94702
G.P.O. Box 3234
New York, N.Y.   10001

Third World features and shorts

Time/Life Films
43 W. 16th Street
New York, N.Y.   10011

BBC TV films, documentaries,
educational

Times Film Corp.
144 W. 57th Street
New York, N.Y.   10019

35mm only, few foreign features;
mainly sexploitation

Toho International
1501 Broadway
New York, N.Y.   10036

Japanese films, 35mm

Tower Films
8400 Sunset Boulevard
Los Angeles, Calif.   90069

35mm independent features, also
35mm commercial films for
non-theatrical use

Twyman Films
329 Salem Avenue
Dayton, Ohio   45406

American and foreign features

United Artists/16mm Division
729 Seventh Avenue
New York, N.Y.   10019
35mm Division:
300 Goldengate Avenue
San Francisco, Calif.   94102

United Artists features, American and
foreign, also classics and shorts

United Films, Inc.
2903 Louisiana Street
Houston, Texas   77066
1122 South Cheyenne
Tulsa, Okla.   74119

American and foreign features and
shorts, serials

United Film Enterprises
1546 Broadway
New York, N.Y.   10036

German films; 35mm also

United Productions of America, Inc.
600 Madison Avenue
New York, N.Y.   10036

UPA cartoons, American features

United World Films
221 Park Avenue South
New York, N.Y.   10003

Free-loan educational, documentary
and travel films

*Universal Kinetic, Education
and Visual Arts*
221 Park Avenue South
New York, N.Y.   10003

American and foreign features, shorts,
classics

Universal/16
205 Walton Street, N.W.
Atlanta, Georgia   30303
425 N. Michigan Avenue
Chicago, Ill.   60611
2001 South Vermont Avenue
Los Angeles, Calif.   90007
630 Ninth Avenue
New York, N.Y.   10036

American and foreign features, shorts, classics

Walter Reade/16
241 East 34th Street
New York, N.Y.   10016

American and foreign features

Warhol Factory
33 Union Square West
New York, N.Y.   10003

Andy Warhol films.
At date of this printing, please book through
Film-Makers Coop,
175 Lexington Avenue,
New York, N.Y.   10016

Warner Brothers Non-Theatrical Division
4000 Warner Boulevard
Burbank, Calif.   91505

Warner Bros. features, American and foreign classics; 16mm and 35mm

Westcoast Films
25 Lusk Street
San Francisco, Calif.   94107

American features, shorts, silents, comedies

Clem Williams Films
2240 Noblestown Road
Pittsburgh, Pa.   15205
5424 West North Avenue
Chicago, Ill.   60639

American features, silents, serials, shorts

Willoughby/Peerless
15 W. 31st Street
New York, N.Y.   10001
415 Lexington Avenue
New York, N.Y.   10017

American features, silents, shorts

Winter Films
405 E. 13th Street
New York, N.Y.   10009

Vietnam veterans against the war documentaries

Woodseye Film Programs
  Allegheny Star Route
  Nevada City, Calif.   95959

Independent and experimental
  "underground" shorts in packages

Youth Film Distribution Center
  43 W. 16th Street
  New York, N.Y.   10011

Films by young film-makers

Zipporah Films, Inc.
  54 Lewis Wharf
  Boston, Mass.   02110

Films of Frederick Wiseman

FILM BOOKSHOPS

U.S.A.

CINEMABILIA, 10 Cornelia St., New York, N.Y. 10014. Tel. 989.8519.
Ernest Burns has made his Cinemabilia into a film buff's paradise, with just about the largest stock of cinema material in New York, including an extensive number of stills, posters, lobby cards, programmes, press books, sheet music, clippings, special articles, and special collections. Personal attention is given to foreign and domestic mail orders, and catalogues (300 pages, $2.50) are issued.

DRAMA BOOKSHOP, 150 West 52nd St., New York, N.Y. 10019. Tel. JU 2.1037.
Arthur Seelen and Allen Collins preside over a most impressive stock of film publications. Drama have also entered the publishing field, with Herman G. Weinberg's *Saint Cinema* (see Book Reviews) and the new *Guide to Film Festivals* ($10). The mail order service at Drama is outstandingly reliable. Write for a catalogue.

GOTHAM BOOK MART, 41 West 47th St., New York, N.Y. 10036.
As its *Film File No. 6* will testify, Gotham has achieved a remarkable pre-eminence in the film bookshop field, and has been flourishing since 1920. Philip Lyman, the General Manager, has worked hard to expand the film section, and as a result the Gotham is a delight for any film buff to visit. Television and radio are also covered, and back numbers of magazines are kept with loving care.

HAMPTON BOOKS, Route 1, Box 76, Newberry, S.C. 29108. Tel. 803.276.6870.
No longer in Hampton Bays, N.Y., this old-established firm does most of its business by mail, and issues a handsome and comprehensive catalogue (*Cinema 6* is now available, price $1). Ben Hamilton and his wife also issue *CTVD*, a quarterly review in English of the serious foreign-language cinema and television press. There are some 25,000 books in stock here, plus a huge selection of *aviation* literature, pictorial material, mss etc.

LARRY EDMUNDS BOOKSHOP, 6658 Hollywood Blvd., Hollywood, California 90028. Tel. 213.463.3273.
A West Coast treasure trove for film buffs, the Larry Edmunds Bookshop has attained its present fame largely due to the efforts of Milton and Git Luboviski and their family. The current catalogue ($2.95) is massive, and includes just about every conceivable film publication (14,500 items), as well as enormous numbers of stills, posters and other memorabilia. Particularly strong on prewar material.

England

FRENCH'S THEATRE BOOKSHOP, 26 Southampton St., London W.C.2.
A firm known throughout the world for its books on the theatre, cinema and television. All books in print on these subjects may be found here.

MOTLEY BOOKS, 10 Westminster Palace Gardens, Artillery Row, London S.W.1. Tel. 828.8931.
Barbara Cavanagh is one of the few film booksellers who has an enormous amount of cinema and pre-cinema material, including optical toys and new foreign books in unusual languages. Readers in London should note that business is by appointment only.

ZWEMMER, A., 78 Charing Cross Rd., London W.C.2. Tel. 836.4710.
Zwemmers are probably the widest known of all British film bookshops, and are also the publishers of the *International Film Guide* Series and *Screen* Series. Their shop always contains the latest British and foreign film magazines, as well as books from several countries. There is a large postal department, and the catalogues are excellent.

Canada

CINE BOOKS, 692a Yonge St., Toronto; Ontario. Tel. 964.6474.
David Beard and his friends have worked like Trojans to establish Cine Books as *the* Canadian centre for film books. Their stock is attractively arranged in the shop, but they also provide a most efficient mail order service (send for a catalogue at $1). Stills, posters, memorabilia, and the entire range of contemporary film literature can be obtained.

INDEX